SpringerBriefs in Modern Perspectives on Disability Research

Series Editors

Gabriel Bennett, Independent Researcher, Klemzig, Australia

Emma Goodall, Healthy Possibilities, Seaford, Australia

This book series on disability research is a comprehensive collection of research on disability and related issues. The series is designed to promote interdisciplinary collaboration and exchange, bringing together scholars and practitioners from different fields to share their perspectives and insights. Disability research is an interdisciplinary field that examines the social, cultural, historical, and political dimensions of disability. It encompasses a wide range of topics, including disability rights, accessibility, assistive technologies, healthcare, education, employment, and social welfare. Disability research scholars employ a range of theoretical and methodological approaches to understand the experiences of people with disabilities, as well as the ways in which disability intersects with other social identities such as race, gender, sexuality, and class.

The series seeks to advance knowledge and understanding of disability by publishing rigorous, innovative, and relevant research. It aims to promote disability rights and social justice by highlighting the ways in which people with disabilities are marginalized and discriminated against in society, and advocating for greater social inclusion and accessibility. The series also seeks to inform policy and practice by disseminating research findings that can help to shape policy decisions and contribute to positive social change.

Gabriel Bennett

Psilocybin Therapy

Springer

Gabriel Bennett
Adelaide, SA, Australia

ISSN 3004-9709 ISSN 3004-9717 (electronic)
SpringerBriefs in Modern Perspectives on Disability Research
ISBN 978-981-95-4118-8 ISBN 978-981-95-4119-5 (eBook)
https://doi.org/10.1007/978-981-95-4119-5

This Springer imprint is published by the registered company Springer Nature Singapore Pte Ltd.
The registered company address is: 152 Beach Road, #21-01/04 Gateway East, Singapore 189721, Singapore

Statement About the Use of Artificial Intelligence

ChatGPT, a large language model artificial intelligence programme developed by the company OpenAI, was used to enhance the clarity of the concepts articulated in this book. All other procedures that were used to create this book were performed by Dr Gabriel Bennett.

Competing Interests The author has no competing interests to declare that are relevant to the content of this manuscript.

Blurb

Psilocybin—the psychoactive compound in certain mushrooms—is experiencing a revival in psychiatric research, particularly for its potential to treat depression. This book offers a focused, critical synthesis of existing literature reviews that examine psilocybin's therapeutic role in alleviating depressive symptoms. Rather than conducting new experiments, this work distils findings from the broader body of clinical and observational research, as presented in high-quality reviews. It brings together insights from studies that have investigated psilocybin's efficacy in both treatment-resistant and general depression, providing a comprehensive picture of current knowledge in the field. This book presents key themes across the literature: reported improvements in mood and well-being, the rapid onset of therapeutic effects, and the enduring impact of even single-dose sessions. At the same time, it addresses crucial limitations in the research base, including small sample sizes, short follow-up periods, inconsistent methodologies, and questions surrounding placebo controls. The importance of psychological support, participant preparation, and the influence of context are also explored in depth.

Contents

About the Author

Gabriel Bennett, PhD Dr Gabriel Bennett, formally Dr Matthew Bennett, holds a PhD in Disability Studies from Flinders University, South Australia, Australia. He has lectured in Disability Studies at Griffith University, Queensland, Australia. He has also advised the Australian Government's Autism CRC and has published multiple books, including:

- Bennett, G., & Goodall, E. (2024). *The role that assistance dogs play in supporting people with disabilities*. Springer International Publishing AG. https://doi.org/10.1007/978-981-97-1492-6
- Bennett, G. (2024). *Senotherapy: A potential pharmacological strategy for prolonging human Lifespan and Healthspan*. Springer International Publishing AG. https://doi.org/10.1007/978-981-97-3637-9
- Bennett, G. (2024). *A scoping review of clinical studies about the therapeutic benefits of medical cannabis*. Springer International Publishing AG. https://link.springer.com/book/9789819779406
- Bennett, G., & Goodall, E. (2024). *Autistic people with co-occurring psychological conditions: Prevalence and perspectives from autistics, their families, and professionals*. Springer International Publishing AG. https://doi.org/10.1007/978-981-97-0656-3

List of Acronyms

DB-RCTs	Double-blind randomised controlled trials
LSD	Lysergic acid diethylamide
MDD	Major depressive disorder
PAP	Psilocybin-assisted psychotherapy
PRISMA	Preferred Reporting Items for Systematic Reviews and Meta-Analyses
PTSD	Post-traumatic stress disorder
RCTs	Randomised controlled trials
SMD	Standardised mean difference
SSRIs	Selective serotonin reuptake inhibitors
USFDA	United States Food and Drug Administration

List of Figures

List of Tables

Chapter 1
Introduction

1.1 The History of Psilocybin

Psilocybin is a naturally occurring alkaloid that is produced by a variety of mushroom species (Lowe et al., 2021; Passie et al., 2002). These species inhabit many geographical regions, including the United States of America, Southeast Asia, Europe, Mexico, and Central America (Lowe et al., 2021; Nichols, 2020). Notably, *Psilocybe cubensis* is regarded as the most extensively distributed species within the *Psilocybe* genus (Lowe et al., 2021) (see Fig. 1.1).

Despite thousands of years of psychedelic use in religious and recreational contexts, the earliest known written record of psilocybin use, by way of consuming magic mushrooms, can be found in the *Florentine Codex*. This manuscript contains ethnographical research on Mesoamerica, particularly Mexico and the Aztecs, and was compiled between 1529 and 1579 (Lowe et al., 2021) (see Fig. 1.2).

Modern and rigorous scientific studies about psychedelics began in 1938 when Albert Hoffman of Sandoz Laboratories (Basel, Switzerland) synthesised lysergic acid diethylamide (LSD)—translated from the German term "*Lysergsäurediethylamid*". This event is considered the inception of molecular psychiatry and the beginning of the "*first psychedelic renaissance*". It also signified the first documented discovery of an ergot alkaloid derivative with potential medical applications. During this time, LSD was the most extensively studied substance (Lowe et al., 2021; Nichols, 2020; Thomas et al., 2017). Additionally, in 1947, Sandoz Laboratories started selling LSD as a psychiatric medication for neurosis, alcoholism, criminal behaviour, schizophrenia, sexual perversions, autism, and verbal behaviour (Ball & Armstrong, 1961; Bender et al., 1961; Johnson, 1969; Lowe et al., 2021; Ludwig et al., 1969; Sigafoos et al., 2007; Smart & Storm, 1964) (see Fig. 1.2).

In 1957, Albert Hofmann obtained a sample of dried *Psilocybe mexicana* mushrooms from a mycologist based in Huautla de Jiménez, Oaxaca, Mexico—an event

G. Bennett, *Psilocybin Therapy*, SpringerBriefs in Modern Perspectives on Disability Research, https://doi.org/10.1007/978-981-95-4119-5_1

Fig. 1.1 Eleven species of psilocybin-producing mushrooms. *Notes:* (**a**) *Psilocybe cubensis* (Earle) Singer a.k.a. *Stropharia cubensis*. (**b**) *Psilocybe caerulescens* Murrill (a.k.a. Landslide

(continued)

Mushrooms, Derrumbes). (**c**) *Psilocybe mexicana* R. Heim (a.k.a. Teonanacatl, Pajaritos). (**d**) *Psilocybe caerulipes* (Peck) Sacc. (a.k.a. Blue Foot Mushroom). (**e**) *Psilocybe stuntzii* Guzmán and J. Ott (a.k.a. Blue Ringer Mushroom, Stuntz's Blue Legs). (**f**) *Psilocybe cyanescens* Wakef. (a.k.a. Wavy Caps). (**g**) *Psilocybe azurescens* Stamets and Gartz (a.k.a. Flying Saucer Mushrooms). (**h**) *Psilocybe pelliculosa* (A.H. Sm.) Singer and A.H. Sm. (**i**) *Psilocybe tampanensis* Guzmán and Pollock (a.k.a. Magic Truffles, Philosopher's Stone. (**j**) *Psilocybe baeocystis* Singer and A.H. Sm. (**k**) *Psilocybe hoogshagenii R. Heim nom. inval.* (a.k.a. Little Birds of the Woods). *Source:* Lowe et al. (2021), p. 9

often regarded by those in medical pharmacology as the onset of the so-called "*second psychedelic renaissance*". To verify the mushrooms' psychoactive properties, Hofmann employed paper chromatography to separate the chemical constituents of mushroom extracts, ingesting each fraction to identify the bioactive compound. The psychoactive component was subsequently isolated, chemically characterised and named psilocybin. In 1958, Hofmann and his colleagues at Sandoz Laboratories published both the chemical structure and synthetic pathway of psilocybin, as well as that of psilocin, a minor component identified as the dephosphorylated analogue of psilocybin. During the 1960s, Sandoz Laboratories marketed psilocybin under the trade name Indocybin™, which was supplied in 2 mg oral tablets for psychotherapeutic use. This point in time was defined by exploratory studies into the use of psilocybin as a tool for probing brain function, examining its potential to reduce criminal recidivism, and assessing its role as an entheogen in religious or spiritually inclined populations, such as divinity students (Lowe et al., 2021; Nichols, 2020; Passie et al., 2002) (see Fig. 1.2).

During the 1960s and 1970s, the recreational use of psychedelic substances became a defining feature of the "*hippie*" counterculture movement in the United States of America. This cultural association played a significant role in prompting the United States Drug Enforcement Administration to classify several psychedelics—including LSD, N,N-dimethyltryptamine, psilocybin, and mescaline—as Schedule I substances under the Controlled Substances Act of 1970. The connection between psychedelics and the countercultural movement, which was often sensationalised in public discourse, contributed to the enduring stigmatisation of these compounds. This stigma has historically impeded scientific inquiry and the progression of research into the therapeutic potential of psychedelic substances—a trend that has only recently begun to reverse (Lowe et al., 2021) (see Fig. 1.2).

Historically, the pharmaceutical industry—mirroring broader societal perceptions and regulatory attitudes—largely dismissed psychedelic research. However, in recent years, there has been an increased interest in this field, with a growing body of clinical studies indicating the potential efficacy of psilocybin-assisted therapy as an adjunct to conventional psychotherapy (Kargbo, 2020). Early investigations into hallucinogens documented the therapeutic application of LSD in managing the resistant behavioural symptoms associated with early infantile autism and childhood schizophrenia (Hoch et al., 1952; Kargbo, 2020; Lowe et al., 2021; Simmons Iii et al., 1966). By the 1960s, more than 40,000 individuals had participated in psychedelic research trials, although many of these studies were conducted using

6000-7000 years ago	Thousands of years of religious use of magic mushrooms by Old-World cultures (mushroom-worshipping ceremonies).
1579	Earliest known record of magic mushroom use in the *Florentine Codex* (a manuscript of ethno-graphical research of Mesoamerica, particularly of Mexico and the Aztecs, compiled between 1529 and 1579.
1897	Isolation of Mescaline from the Peyote cactus by Arthur Heffter.
1922	PCP synthesized.
1938	Beginning of the "First Psychedelic Renaissance". Scientist Albert Hoffman of Sandoz Laboratories (Basel, Switzerland) synthesizes Lysergic Acid Diethylamide (LSD).
1943	Albert Hoffman takes LSD for the first time & discovers its psychedelic effects.
1947	First LSD studies humans. Sandoz begins marketing and distributing LSD as a psychiatric drug for the treatment of alcoholism and neurosis. This halted in 1965.
1952	Dr. Charles Savage publishes the first study on the use of LSD to treat depression.
1957	Dr. Gordon Wasson publishes article on Magic Mushrooms in Life magazine.
1958	Albert Hoffman and colleagues elucidate the structure and synthesis of Psilocybin from a sample of dried *Psilocybe mexicana* mushrooms from Huautla de Jiménez (Oaxaca, Mexico).
1960-1970	- "Second Psychedelic Renaissance" - Ketamine synthesized (1962) - The U.S. government approves Peyote as a religious sacrament in the Native American Church of America. - Growing association of psychedelics to "hippie" counter culture. Growing negative stigmatization of psychedelics. - Distribution of INDOCYBIN®, a psycho-therapeutic drug, by Sandoz Pharmaceuticals (Basel, Switzerland). - First study conducted on the effects of psychedelic drugs on schizophrenics (Spring Grove Experiment 1963-1976).
1970	Prohibition of Hallucinogens (Schedule 1 classification)
2004	- Beginning of the "Third Psychedelic Renaissance". - UCLA researchers begin clinical trials on psilocybin for the treatment of pain, anxiety and depression in patients with advanced-stage cancer.
2006	Researchers at John's Hopkins begin phenomenological studies on psilocybin use.
2012	First psilocybin function magnetic resonance neuro-imaging (fMRI) study.
2018	- Compass Pathways Ltd (London, United Kingdom) receives FDA approval of "breakthrough therapy" status in 2018 for a psilocybin treatment they developed for treatment-resistant depression. - FDA approval of SPRAVATO®, a ketamine analog developed by Johnson and Johnson for use in patients suffering from treatment-resistant depression.
2019	- Usona Institute receives FDA "breakthrough therapy" status for a psilocybin treatment for major depressive disorder (MDD)
2020-present	- John's Hopkins University builds the Center for Psychedelic & Consciousness research, the first of its kind (September 2020). - The Icahn School of Medicine at Mount Sinai launches The Center for Psychedelic Psychotherapy and Trauma Research (January 2021).

Fig. 1.2 Historical timeline of psychedelic substances. *Source:* Lowe et al. (2021), p. 6.

flawed methodological standards by contemporary criteria (Lowe et al., 2021) (see Fig. 1.2).

In 2004, researchers at the University of California, Los Angeles, initiated clinical trials investigating the use of psilocybin for alleviating pain, anxiety, and depression in patients with advanced-stage cancer. This development is often regarded as marking the onset of the "*third psychedelic renaissance*". A pivotal 2006 publication by Johns Hopkins University played a central role in revitalising global interest in psychedelic science, contributing to the establishment of the university's dedicated Psychedelic Research Unit (Griffiths et al., 2006). This initiative subsequently evolved into the Center for Psychedelic and Consciousness Research, which, since its founding in 2006, has produced over eighty peer-reviewed publications on psychedelic substances. In September 2020, Johns Hopkins University formally inaugurated the Center for Psychedelic and Consciousness Research, the first institution of its kind devoted exclusively to this field (Lowe et al., 2021) (see Fig. 1.2).

In conjunction with the resurgence of academic interest in psychedelic research, pharmaceutical engagement in the field has markedly increased. In 2018, Compass Pathways Ltd., based in London, United Kingdom, obtained "*breakthrough therapy*" status from the United States Food and Drug Administration (USFDA) for a psilocybin-based treatment targeting treatment-resistant depression. During the same year, the USFDA also approved SPRAVATO®, a ketamine derivative developed by Johnson & Johnson, for use in patients with treatment-resistant depression. Subsequently, in 2019, the Usona Institute was granted USFDA "*breakthrough therapy*" status for its psilocybin formulation intended for the treatment of major depressive disorder. To date, more than 27,000 scientific publications have addressed psychedelic compounds, with over 1,000 focusing specifically on psilocybin. At present, psilocybin is the most extensively studied psychedelic substance (Johnson & Griffiths, 2017; Lowe et al., 2021) (see Fig. 1.2).

1.2 The Therapeutic Potential of Psilocybin

According to the 2017 Global Drug Survey, it was estimated that approximately 20.6% of the global population who had used drugs of any type had decided to use psilocybin-producing mushrooms within their lifetime. This book will focus on psilocybin, the primary psychoactive component of these mushrooms, which has been utilised for thousands of years in ceremonial practices by ancient cultures. In addition to the well-documented recreational, spiritual, and religious uses of psilocybin-producing mushrooms, there is considerable medicinal value, as evidenced by anecdotal reports and scientific studies (Lowe et al., 2021). Table 1.1 outlines the diseases in which psilocybin-assisted therapy is currently being investigated.

Table 1.1 Psilocybin-assisted therapy for specific conditions

Diseased State/Condition
Alcohol dependence
Stimulant dependence
Cocaine addiction
Tobacco addiction
Nicotine addiction
Opioid addiction
Cannabis dependence
Anxiety disorders such as: 1. Post-traumatic stress disorder, 2. Generalised anxiety disorder, 3. Obsessive–compulsive disorder 4. Advanced-stage cancer-related anxiety 5. Psychological distress associated with existential crisis of terminal disease 6. Adjustment disorder with anxiety
Cancer-related depression
Treatment-resistant depression
Major depressive disorder
Severe existential depression
Suicidality (ideation and actual attempts)
Cluster ("suicide") headaches
Chronic pain
Intractable phantom pain
Demoralisation
Demoralisation in older, long-term AIDS survivor men
Dysfunctional social cognition
Maladaptive narcissism
Borderline personality disorder
Narcissistic personality disorder
Epilepsy
Psychopathy
Emotional dysregulation and violence against one's partner
Inflammation

Source: Lowe et al. (2021), p. 4

1.3 Government-Funded Research About Psilocybin

Currently, there are many government-funded research projects into the therapeutic benefits of psilocybin therapy. Table 1.2 lists a range of clinical trials investigating the therapeutic potential of psilocybin for various mental health and neurological conditions. While major depressive disorder and treatment-resistant depression are the most common targets, several studies also explore psilocybin's effects in

Table 1.2 Active clinical trials of psilocybin, as of December 2024, in ClinicalTrials.gov

Study Title	NCT Number	Condition(s)	Intervention(s)
Effect of Psilocybin Only and Psilocybin Assisted Cognitive Behavioural Therapy in the Management of Major Depressive Disorder and Associated Metabolic, Immune, Inflammatory, Neuroplasticity and Electrical Activity Markers	NCT06746441	Major depressive disorder	Psilocybin, Behavioural cognitive therapy
Psilocybin for Treatment-Resistant Depression in Autism With Pre-Post Brain and Cognitive Measurement to Understand Mechanisms	NCT06731621	Treatment-resistant depression, Autism spectrum disorder	Psilocybin
Acceptability & Safety of Two Sequential Doses of Psilocybin in Bipolar Disorder II Depression	NCT06706232	Bipolar II disorder, Bipolar depression, Suicidality	Psilocybin, Therapeutic support
Effect of Psilocybin on the Positive Valence System in Treatment-resistant Depression	NCT06650800	Treatment-resistant depression	Psilocybin
Psilocybin Mechanism of Action	NCT06592833	Major depressive disorder	Psilocybin, Pimavanserin, Placebo
Treatment With Psilocybin for Chronic Neuropathic Pain and Depression	NCT06518720	Treatment-resistant depression, Chronic pain	Psilocybin 25 mg
Imaging the Effects of Serotonin 2A Receptor Modulation on Synaptic Density in Treatment-resistant Depression	NCT06512220	Treatment-resistant depression	Psilocybin 25 mg, Risperidone 1 mg
Investigation to Understand and Optimise Psilocybin	NCT06512194	Depression	Psilocybin, Transcutaneous Auricular Vagus Nerve Stimulation (taVNS), Sham taNVS
Neurobiological Effects of Psilocybin in Treatment-Resistant Bipolar Depression	NCT06506019	Bipolar depression	Psilocybin
Psilocybin Therapy for Depression in Parkinson's Disease	NCT06455293	Depression, Parkinson's disease	Psilocybin
Psilocybin-assisted Therapy for Alcohol Use Disorder	NCT06444243	Alcohol use disorder, Alcohol dependence, Depression	Psilocybin, Niacin

(continued)

Table 1.2 (continued)

Study Title	NCT Number	Condition(s)	Intervention(s)
Psilocybin for Hospitalised Patients With Treatment-resistant Depression	NCT06378229	Treatment-resistant depression	Psilocybin
Low-Income Group Psilocybin-Assisted Therapy for Depression	NCT06372197	Depression	Psilocybin
Psilocybin in Chronic Low Back Pain and Depression	NCT06355414	Chronic low back pain, Depression	Psilocybin, Placebo, Supportive therapy sessions
Psilocybin-Assisted Psychotherapy for Treatment-Resistant Depression: Comparing One Versus Two Doses of Psilocybin	NCT06341426	Major depressive disorder, Depression, Treatment-resistant depression	Single psychedelic dose psilocybin, Two psychedelic doses psilocybin
Cancer-Related Major Depression Treated With a Single Dose of Psilocybin	NCT06319378	Major depressive disorder	Psilocybin 25 mg, Psilocybin 1 mg
Psilocybin for Major Depressive Disorder	NCT06308653	Major depressive disorder	Psilocybin 25 mg, Psilocybin 5 mg, Placebo
Psilocybin-Assisted Therapy in Treatment-Resistant Depression	NCT06303739	Refractory depression, Treatment-resistant depression	Psilocybin
The Effects of Psilocybin on Self-Focus and Self-Related Processing in Major Depressive Disorder	NCT06247839	Major depressive disorder	Psilocybin
Psilocybin in Alcohol Use Disorder With Comorbid Depression	NCT06235411	Alcohol-related disorders, Depressive disorders, Addiction	Psilocybin therapy, Inactive psilocybin therapy
Psilocybin for Treatment-Resistant Depression	NCT06230757	Major depressive disorder, Anhedonia, Treatment-resistant depression	Psilocybin 25 mg, Psilocybin (active placebo)
Psilocybin-Assisted Psychotherapy in Patients With Advanced Cancer on Maintenance Therapy	NCT06200155	Depression, Anxiety, Advanced cancer	Psilocybin, Niacin

Study Title	NCT Number	Condition(s)	Intervention(s)
Evaluation of Psilocybin-Assisted Psychotherapy in Treating Severe Depression in Patients With Post-traumatic Stress Disorder	NCT06141876	Post-traumatic stress disorder, Depression	APEX-002-A02, Placebo
Psilocybin rTMS for Treatment-Resistant Depression	NCT06132178	Treatment-resistant depression, Major depressive disorder	Psilocybin, Accelerated intermittent theta burst, Low-dose psilocybin
A Randomised Neuroimaging Trial of Psilocybin in Depression	NCT06072898	Major depressive disorder	Psilocybin
A Phase 2, Randomised, Double-Blind, Placebo-Controlled Study to Evaluate the Efficacy and Safety of up to Two Doses of Psilocybin for the Treatment of Major Depressive Disorder in Adults With Cancer	NCT05947383	Cancer, Major depressive disorder	Psilocybin, Placebo
A Phase II, Multicentre, Randomised, Double-blind, Controlled Study to Investigate the Safety, Tolerability, Pharmacokinetics, and Efficacy of COMP360 in Participants With Recurrent Major Depressive Disorder	NCT05733546	Major depressive disorder	Psilocybin

Source: Erkizia-Santamaría et al. (2025), p. 8

populations with bipolar disorder, chronic pain, autism, post-traumatic stress disorder, alcohol use disorder, and Parkinson's disease. Many trials combine psilocybin with adjunctive interventions, such as cognitive behavioural therapy, neuromodulation, or supportive psychotherapy. Others incorporate neuroimaging and biomarker analysis to better understand psilocybin's mechanisms of action. Together, these studies reflect a growing scientific interest in psilocybin as a novel treatment option, with particular attention to its safety, efficacy, and long-term impact on emotional and cognitive functioning (see Table 1.2) (Erkizia-Santamaría et al., 2025).

1.4 Economic Overview of the Psilocybin Market

In the second quarter of 2019, over USD 320 million was invested in psychedelic neuropharmaceutical development, followed by approximately USD 100 million directed towards psychedelic research and clinical trials in the third quarter. The global psychedelic therapeutics market is projected to grow from USD 2 billion in 2019 to USD 6.8 billion by 2027, with a compound annual growth rate of 16.3%. Recent regulatory advances, such as the FDA approval of SPRAVATO®, a ketamine analogue for treatment-resistant depression, and the breakthrough therapy designation for psilocybin treatments for major depressive disorder by Compass Pathways Ltd. and the Usona Institute, are expected to further stimulate psychedelic research and market growth. Additionally, Numinus Wellness Inc.'s receipt of the first Health Canada licence to cultivate and extract psilocybin is a milestone that will promote the development of synthetic psilocybin, enable rigorous scientific evaluation, and support large-scale production alongside standardised cultivation and extraction methodologies (Lowe et al., 2021).

1.5 Research Questions

To investigate the literature about the impact of psilocybin therapy in the treatment of depression, the following research questions were used to examine the literature collected for this book:

- *Research question 1:* What therapeutic benefits does psilocybin have on treating depression?
  Justification: Depression is a leading global health issue, and many individuals do not respond to standard treatments. Emerging evidence suggests psilocybin may offer significant therapeutic benefits, including rapid and sustained symptom relief. Investigating its effectiveness is crucial to expanding treatment options, guiding clinical practice, and informing mental health policy.
- *Research question 2:* What design limitations exist within the research about the therapeutic benefits of psilocybin in treating depression?

- *Justification:* As interest in psilocybin therapy grows, it is essential to critically assess the design limitations of existing research. Identifying methodological weaknesses—such as small samples, limited follow-up, or lack of controls—helps clarify the strength of current evidence and informs the development of more rigorous studies in the future. This ensures that clinical and policy decisions are based on reliable and generalisable findings.
- *Research question 3:* What are some future directions for research about the usage of psilocybin in the treatment of depression?
  Justification: As psilocybin research advances, identifying future directions is crucial for addressing current gaps and refining therapeutic applications. Exploring unanswered questions—such as optimal dosing, long-term effects, diverse populations, and combination with other treatments—can guide more effective, safe, and inclusive mental health interventions. This research question ensures that the field progresses in a focused and clinically meaningful way.

1.6 Search Procedures

On 11 June 2025, a search for relevant citations indexed on PubMed that could answer the research questions was conducted. It was possible to search for relevant citations that were published by specific academic publishers (e.g., Springer Nature, SAGE, and Routledge). This approach, however, was deemed to be ineffective because several of these publishers had limited search functionality (e.g., unable to restrict the date range of the retrieved citations). Consequently, searching via PubMed was deemed effective because it was possible to search the citation's title and limit the publication date. Additionally, a PubMed search included citations from publishers that were unfamiliar to the researcher.

A Preferred Reporting Items for Systematic Reviews and Meta-Analyses (PRISMA) approach was used to search and examine the citations retrieved from PubMed. PRISMA is an established and widely used approach for collecting, examining, and identifying studies that answer a study's research questions from a large sample of retrieved literature. The PRISMA approach has five steps. These five steps and their relation to this study are listed below.

- *STEP ONE*: The first step involved searching PubMed for literature reviews about psilocybin. The search phrases (*"psilocybin* "[Title]) AND (*"review"*[Title]) were used to retrieve studies.
- *STEP TWO*: The second step involved removing any duplicate records that were retrieved from the single search of PubMed. No duplicate records were identified.
- *STEP THREE*: The third step involved examining each systematic literature review's title and abstract to determine if it answered this book's research questions. Additionally, citations that were retractions, corrections, letters to the editor, or commentaries were not examined for this book.
- STEP FOUR: The fourth step involved reading the entire text of the systematic literature review that was provisionally deemed to answer any of the research questions.

- STEP FIVE: The fifth and final step involved summarising and explaining the results from the systematic literature reviews that were retained from the fourth step in the PRISMA analysis process.

1.7 Methodological Strengths and Weaknesses

1.7.1 Methodological Weaknesses

1.7.1.1 Risk of Omitting Emerging or Niche Topics

Systematic literature reviews require considerable time to complete and publish, which means they often do not contain studies that explain the latest research developments. Consequently, recent discoveries, innovative interventions, or emerging theoretical frameworks may be absent from examined reviews. Likewise, specialised or underexplored areas—such as psilocybin therapy among minority groups or studies employing intersectional approaches—are often overlooked, resulting in notable gaps in the synthesised evidence. Thus, the literature critiqued in this book does not entirely explore the literature about the therapeutic benefits of psilocybin for treating depression.

1.7.1.2 Loss of Primary Data Nuance

Systematic literature reviews are summaries of multiple primary studies, often condensed to fit standardised formats. This results in a significant loss of detail—especially regarding the contextual or procedural aspects of individual trials. For example, reviews may report that a particular dosage of psilocybin was effective in reducing depression scores, but may omit critical elements such as:

- The setting (e.g., presence of a guide, use of music, or room design),
- Patient preparation and integration processes,
- Variability in therapist experience or rapport, and
- Participant narratives or unexpected emotional responses.

These aspects are required to fully understand the therapeutic effect and risks of psilocybin, particularly given its reliance on "*set and setting*" and its capacity to evoke deeply personal or transformative experiences.

1.7.1.3 Dependence on Inclusion Criteria of Reviews

Systematic literature reviews have their own inclusion and exclusion criteria, often designed to ensure internal validity. However, this introduces a selection bias and, therefore, limits the generalisability of the results. For instance, many reviews:

- Exclude studies not published in English,
- Focus only on randomised controlled trials, ignoring real-world or observational data,
- Disregard studies with mixed interventions or diverse patient groups, and
- Ignore qualitative or case study designs.

This bias can exclude relevant, diverse, or emerging forms of evidence, especially in a field like psychedelic research where many early studies and grey literature reports contain valuable insights. Relying solely on reviews reinforces the prejudices and boundaries built into their design.

1.7.1.4 Limited Responsiveness to Emerging Evidence

Systematic literature reviews take time to conduct and publish, often trailing behind current research developments. In a rapidly evolving field of research like psychedelic therapy—where new clinical trials, regulatory changes, and novel delivery models are emerging—reviews may already contain outdated research by the time they are published. Additionally, systematic literature reviews might not contain cutting-edge evidence, such as newly registered trials. Limiting analysis to already published systematic literature reviews may result in a book that has not considered current practice or evolving consensus.

1.7.1.5 Potential for Conflicting Conclusions

Different systematic literature reviews can analyse overlapping data but arrive at divergent conclusions. For instance, some may report strong evidence for psilocybin's efficacy in treating depression, while others—depending on criteria, statistical thresholds, or weighting of outliers—may be more cautious or inconclusive. Relying solely on examining systematic reviews may present the researcher or reader with confusing or contradictory findings, without the opportunity to revisit original studies to evaluate the differences. Without primary source analysis, it is difficult to reconcile these contradictions or to understand the root of the divergence, such as sample heterogeneity, differences in endpoints, or reviewer bias.

1.7.1.6 Methodological Rigour Varies Widely

Systematic literature reviews are not inherently rigorous; their quality can vary widely depending on how they are conducted. Poorly designed reviews may lack proper risk of bias assessments, transparent search strategies, clear inclusion criteria, or adequate evaluation of heterogeneity and publication bias. If such reviews include flawed studies or apply inappropriate analytical methods—such as pooling incompatible outcomes—their conclusions may be misleading. Relying on these reviews without critical appraisal risks presenting weak or erroneous evidence under the guise of scholarly authority, which might compromise the credibility of this book's claims.

1.7.1.7 Inattention to Lived Experience and Qualitative Data

Psychedelic therapy can be highly subjective with patients frequently reporting transformative, mystical, or ineffable experiences that are not easily captured by symptom scales or numerical outcomes. However, most systematic literature reviews prioritise quantitative outcomes—such as reductions in depression or anxiety scores—and exclude studies that base their results on subjective experiences by participants. This means that the subjective dimensions of psilocybin use—emotional breakthroughs, spiritual insights, ego dissolution, and integration challenges—are systematically excluded. Examining only systematic literature reviews will likely overlook these personal dimensions.

1.7.1.8 Risk of Oversimplification and Misleading Generalisations

By their nature, systematic literature reviews condense complex, heterogeneous findings into singular narratives or effect sizes. While this simplifies the task of drawing conclusions, it also carries the risk of oversimplification. For example, a systematic literature review might report that psilocybin has a medium-to-large effect size for reducing depression—but this hides:

- Variability in participant diagnoses (e.g., major depressive disorder vs. cancer-related distress),
- Differences in therapeutic frameworks (e.g., psychodynamic vs. supportive models),
- Cultural or legal contexts (e.g., Indigenous use vs. Western medical models), and
- Variations in integration and aftercare.

Such generalisations can mislead readers into thinking psilocybin therapy is uniformly effective, rather than context-sensitive and variable in its impact. The richness and complexity of the field may be lost in pursuit of a succinct statistical summary.

1.7.1.9 Summary

In summary, while focusing on systematic reviews and meta-analyses can provide a clear, evidence-based overview of psilocybin therapy, it risks simplifying complexity, overlooking nuance, and reinforcing existing biases. A more comprehensive and credible account of the field could occur by combining these high-level syntheses with the broader sociocultural and ethical dimensions of psychedelic use. This layered approach can better capture the full scope of what psilocybin therapy entails—and what it might promise.

1.7.2 Methodological strengths

Reviewing only systematic literature reviews has several methodological strengths, particularly in fields like psilocybin therapy where individual studies vary widely in design, quality, and outcomes. This high-level approach brings several benefits in terms of rigour, efficiency, and evidence synthesis, which can support robust conclusions about broad patterns in the literature. Below is a detailed account of the strengths associated with examining only systematic literature reviews about psilocybin usage.

1.7.2.1 Identification of Research Gaps and Inconsistencies

One of the defining strengths of systematic literature reviews is their ability to uncover limitations in existing research. These reviews frequently end by pointing out gaps in knowledge, methodological shortcomings, or populations that are insufficiently represented. Consequently, they are particularly valuable for identifying areas requiring extra study and highlighting ongoing inconsistencies. This book draws on such findings to outline the current limits of knowledge about psilocybin research and suggest avenues for future exploration.

1.7.2.2 Time Efficiency and Manageability

Due to the expansive nature of psilocybin research, reviewing every primary study would have been both unrealistic and unmanageable. Limiting the scope of the analysis to systematic literature reviews greatly simplifies this task. These sources have already distilled and critically assessed primary research, enabling readers to construct a clear and cohesive synthesis without being overwhelmed by the volume and diversity of individual studies.

1.7.2.3 Aggregation of Evidence Across Multiple Studies

One of the key strengths of systematic literature reviews is their ability to combine findings from numerous primary studies, thereby increasing statistical power and improving the precision of treatment effect estimates. This approach is particularly valuable in psilocybin therapy research, where individual studies are often small or exploratory. By pooling data, systematic literature reviews can detect subtle effects, provide more reliable estimates of efficacy for conditions such as depression, anxiety, post-traumatic stress disorder (PTSD), and substance use disorders, and assess the consistency of results across different studies.

1.7.2.4 Systematic and Transparent Methodology

Systematic literature reviews use structured, transparent, and replicable processes to identify, select, and assess studies, typically involving pre-defined inclusion criteria, comprehensive database searches, bias assessments, and standardised data extraction methods. These rigorous procedures minimise selection bias and enhance the reliability and reproducibility of findings. As a result, systematic literature reviews serve as a cornerstone of evidence-based practice, offering a dependable framework for evaluating the clinical utility of interventions like psilocybin therapy.

1.7.2.5 Reduction of Random Error and Study-Level Variability

By pooling data from multiple trials, systematic literature reviews help reduce the impact of random variation and outliers that may distort findings in individual studies. Small sample sizes or unique study conditions can produce extreme results, but aggregating these outcomes smooths out anomalies and reduces random error. This process enhances the generalisability of conclusions about treatment effectiveness. In psychedelic research—where outcomes are highly sensitive to factors like participant expectations, setting, and therapist interaction—this capacity to contextualise and average disparate findings is particularly valuable.

1.7.2.6 Ability to Identify Patterns and Moderators

Advanced meta-analytic techniques, such as subgroup analysis and meta-regression, enable researchers to identify moderator variables that account for variability in effect sizes across studies. In the context of psilocybin therapy these methods can reveal, for example, that efficacy is stronger in randomised controlled trials than in observational studies, more pronounced for depression than anxiety, or influenced by factors like dose, session number, and integration therapy. This analytical depth helps refine treatment protocols, guide future research, and move inquiry beyond whether psilocybin works to understanding under what conditions, for whom, and how it is most effective.

1.7.2.7 Assessment of Methodological Quality and Risk of Bias

Systematic literature reviews frequently employ formal tools—such as the Cochrane Risk of Bias tool—to assess the methodological quality and internal validity of included studies. These evaluations help readers interpret findings with appropriate caution by highlighting potential sources of bias. This is especially important in psychedelic research, where studies often contend with methodological challenges like small sample sizes, lack of blinding, expectancy effects, and difficulties in placebo control. Such quality assessments enhance the credibility and interpretability of the evidence base.

1.7.2.8 Efficient Summarisation of Large and Fragmented Literatures

As research on psilocybin therapy expands across various conditions, populations, and methodologies, systematic literature reviews provide an efficient means of synthesising this fragmented evidence base. By distilling large volumes of data into structured, accessible findings, they offer valuable insights for clinicians seeking evidence-based guidance, policymakers evaluating regulatory decisions, ethicists and legal scholars examining broader implications, and researchers identifying knowledge gaps. These reviews enhance the usability of the literature and support informed decision-making in both clinical and policy settings.

1.7.2.9 Foundation for Evidence-Based Recommendations

Due to their methodological rigour and comprehensive synthesis of existing research, systematic literature reviews are often regarded as one of the most rigorous approaches to examining clinical research. They can influence clinical guidelines, informing regulatory decisions, and justifying ethical frameworks or trial designs. For emerging or controversial treatments like psilocybin, relying solely on this level of evidence can significantly enhance the credibility of this book's claims—particularly for audiences who prioritise scientific legitimacy, such as healthcare professionals.

1.7.2.10 Standardisation Across Diverse Studies

Psychedelic trials often vary in outcome measures, dosing protocols, and participant characteristics, making direct comparisons challenging. Meta-analytic techniques address this by standardising findings through common effect size metrics and unified statistical models. This standardisation enables meaningful comparisons across diverse studies, allowing researchers to generate clearer, more interpretable insights than would be possible through narrative reviews alone.

1.7.2.11 Summary

In summary, relying solely on systematic literature reviews to study psilocybin therapy has significant methodological strengths. It provides a rigorous, transparent, and statistically powerful synthesis of the literature. It supports generalisability, highlights broader trends, and enables evidence-based conclusions while minimising some forms of bias inherent in primary studies.

While this approach has limitations—such as a tendency to not include emerging data—it offers a robust foundation for clinical, ethical, and policy discussions. In a field as emotionally and politically charged as psychedelic research, anchoring the discussion in high-quality aggregated evidence can be a deliberate and defensible choice.

1.8 Intended Audience for This Book

1.8.1 Medical and Mental Health Professionals

Psychiatrists, psychologists, general practitioners, and other mental health professionals would be interested in this book due to the growing body of research suggesting psilocybin's potential as a treatment for depression, anxiety, PTSD, addiction, and existential distress in palliative care. These professionals may be looking to expand their understanding of alternative or emerging treatment modalities, especially those backed by clinical trials. This book can provide critical insights into psilocybin's therapeutic potential in clinical practice or treatment models in the future.

1.8.2 Researchers and Academics

Scholars in disciplines such as neuroscience, pharmacology, psychology, anthropology, and religious studies might find value in this book. Academic researchers are often interested in methodological rigour, the quality of evidence, and gaps in the literature. A book that examined systematic literature reviews of psilocybin therapy would be particularly useful as a reference tool, offering both an overview of the evidence base and a springboard for future research questions. It could also appeal to those studying consciousness, spirituality, or the therapeutic effects of altered states.

1.8.3 Policy Makers and Regulators

Government officials, policy analysts, and legal professionals concerned with drug legislation and mental health policy would benefit from a grounded, evidence-based presentation of psilocybin's therapeutic potential. As interest in psychedelic-assisted therapy grows and jurisdictions around the world begin to reconsider their legal frameworks for psychedelics, this book—which outlines the scientific consensus, risks, benefits, and regulatory models—can support informed decision-making.

1.8.4 Students in Health, Psychology, or Drug Policy

Undergraduate and postgraduate students—especially those who are studying medicine, psychology, social work, pharmacology, or public policy—could use this book as an educational resource. A synthesis of high-quality reviews would help them understand the key debates and developments in psychedelic research. For students writing dissertations or essays, this book could provide a concise yet comprehensive starting point that distils complex research into accessible summaries.

1.8.5 Therapists and Psychedelic-Assisted Therapy Practitioners

Professionals working directly in the field of psychedelic-assisted therapy, or those training to become certified in it, would benefit from this book because it offers outcomes from established trials. This group is likely to be especially interested in patient experiences, therapeutic mechanisms (such as emotional breakthrough or ego dissolution), and guidance on preparation, dosing, and integration. This book can serve as both a practical and theoretical resource to deepen their understanding of the nuances of psilocybin therapy.

1.8.6 General Public with an Interest in Psychedelics or Self-Exploration

Readers with a curiosity about psychedelics—whether for personal growth, mental health, or spiritual exploration—may be drawn to this book for its clarity, depth, and grounding in scientific evidence. This audience often values balanced, jargon-free information that addresses both the promises and the risks of psilocybin use. This book offers historical context, therapeutic case studies, and explanations of the science in plain language that can help them make sense of the rapidly evolving public discourse on psychedelics.

1.9 Description of Upcoming Chapters

1.9.1 Chapter 2: Therapeutic Benefits of Psilocybin in Treating Depression

In recent years, there has been a resurgence of scientific interest in psilocybin as a promising therapeutic agent for depression, particularly treatment-resistant depression and depression linked to serious medical conditions. Following decades of restricted research due to legal barriers, accumulating clinical trials and meta-analyses now indicate that psilocybin, especially when administered alongside psychotherapy, can produce rapid, significant, and sustained reductions in depressive symptoms. Studies consistently report a favourable safety profile with few serious adverse effects, distinguishing psilocybin from conventional antidepressants, such as selective serotonin reuptake inhibitors. Nevertheless, key gaps remain, including the need for standardised psychotherapeutic frameworks, optimised dosing strategies, and large-scale, placebo-controlled trials to verify long-term efficacy and safety. While current evidence positions psilocybin as a potentially transformative psychiatric treatment, further rigorous investigation is essential to fully define its clinical applications and optimise therapeutic protocols.

1.9.2 Chapter 3: Current Research Limitations and Opportunities for Studying Psilocybin's Therapeutic Benefits in Treating Depression

As scientific interest in psilocybin therapy accelerates, an expanding body of research has emerged exploring its potential to treat depression and related mental health disorders. Although early results are encouraging, a detailed analysis reveals numerous methodological shortcomings that undermine the reliability, reproducibility, and generalisability of current findings. This chapter provides a critical overview of common limitations identified in recent systematic reviews, meta-analyses, and primary clinical studies. These challenges—including small sample sizes, varied study designs, insufficient blinding, and incomplete reporting of key variables—hinder the establishment of rigorous, evidence-based treatment guidelines. By highlighting these issues and proposing strategies to address them, this chapter seeks to guide future research efforts and enhance methodological standards within psychedelic science.

1.9.3 Chapter 4: Conclusion

The final chapter of this book summarises the gaps in our existing literature. Its purpose is to summarise this field of research.

References

Ball, J. R., & Armstrong, J. J. (1961). The use of L.S.D. 25 (D-lysergic acid diethylamide) in the treatment of the sexual perversions. *Canadian Psychiatric Association journal, 6*, 231–235. https://doi.org/10.1177/070674376100600407

Bender, L., Goldschmidt, L., & Sankar, D. V. (1961). Treatment of autistic schizophrenic children with LSD-25 and UML-491. *Recent Advances in Biological Psychiatry, 4*, 170–179. https://doi.org/10.1007/978-1-4684-8306-2_17

Erkizia-Santamaría, I., Horrillo, I., Meana, J. J., & Ortega, J. E. (2025). Clinical and pre-clinical evidence of psilocybin as antidepressant. A narrative review. *Progress in Neuro-Psychopharmacology & Biological Psychiatry, 136*, 111249. https://doi.org/10.1016/j.pnpbp.2025.111249

Griffiths, R. R., Richards, W. A., McCann, U., & Jesse, R. (2006). Psilocybin can occasion mystical-type experiences having substantial and sustained personal meaning and spiritual significance. *Psychopharmacology, 187*(3), 268–292. https://doi.org/10.1007/s00213-006-0457-5

Hoch, P. H., Cattell, J. P., & Pennes, H. H. (1952). Effects of mescaline and lysergic acid (d-LSD-25). *The American Journal of Psychiatry, 108*(8), 579–584. https://doi.org/10.1176/ajp.108.8.579

Johnson, F. G. (1969). LSD in the treatment of alcoholism. *The American Journal of Psychiatry, 126*(4), 481–487. https://doi.org/10.1176/ajp.126.4.481

Johnson, M. W., & Griffiths, R. R. (2017). Potential therapeutic effects of psilocybin. *Neurotherapeutics: The Journal of the American Society for Experimental Neuro Therapeutics, 14*(3), 734–740. https://doi.org/10.1007/s13311-017-0542-y

Kargbo, R. B. (2020). Psilocybin Therapeutic Research: The Present and Future Paradigm. *ACS Medicinal Chemistry Letters, 11*(4), 399–402. https://doi.org/10.1021/acsmedchemlett.0c00048

Lowe, H., Toyang, N., Steele, B., Valentine, H., Grant, J., Ali, A., Ngwa, W., & Gordon, L. (2021). The therapeutic potential of psilocybin. *Molecules (Basel, Switzerland), 26*(10), 2948. https://doi.org/10.3390/molecules26102948

Ludwig, A., Levine, J., Stark, L., & Lazar, R. (1969). A clinical study of LSD treatment in alcoholism. *The American Journal of Psychiatry, 126*(1), 59–69. https://doi.org/10.1176/ajp.126.1.59

Nichols, D. E. (2020). Psilocybin: From ancient magic to modern medicine. *The Journal of Antibiotics, 73*(10), 679–686. https://doi.org/10.1038/s41429-020-0311-8

Passie, T., Seifert, J., Schneider, U., & Emrich, H. M. (2002). The pharmacology of psilocybin. *Addiction Biology, 7*(4), 357–364. https://doi.org/10.1080/1355621021000005937

Sigafoos, J., Green, V. A., Edrisinha, C., & Lancioni, G. E. (2007). Flashback to the 1960s: LSD in the treatment of autism. *Developmental Neurorehabilitation, 10*(1), 75–81. https://doi.org/10.1080/13638490601106277

Simmons Iii, J. Q., Leiken, S. J., Lovaas, O. I., Schaeffer, B., & Perloff, B. (1966). Modification of autistic behavior with LSD-25. *American Journal of Psychiatry, 122*(11), 1201–1211. https://doi.org/10.1176/ajp.122.11.1201

Smart, R. G., & Storm, T. (1964). The efficacy of LSD in the treatment of alcoholism. *Quarterly Journal of Studies on Alcohol, 25*, 333–338.

Thomas, K., Malcolm, B., & Lastra, D. (2017). Psilocybin-assisted therapy: A review of a novel treatment for psychiatric disorders. *Journal of Psychoactive Drugs, 49*(5), 446–455. https://doi.org/10.1080/02791072.2017.1320734

Chapter 2
Therapeutic Benefits of Psilocybin in Treating Depression

2.1 Summary of Literature Reviews About Psilocybin's Therapeutic Potential to Treat Depression

Recent years have seen a resurgence in research exploring psilocybin's therapeutic potential, especially for depression. According to van Amsterdam and van den Brink (2022), psychedelic substances were widely used before their prohibition in the United States of America, which significantly hampered scientific inquiry into their effects. However, since the 1990s, interest in their therapeutic applications has grown considerably. van Amsterdam and van den Brink's systematic review examined the clinical efficacy of psilocybin in treating various mental health disorders, focusing exclusively on randomised clinical trials. Their review included 11 studies (15 publications in total), comprising seven randomised controlled trials (RCTs) and four open-label studies, with a combined participant pool of 488 individuals—333 received psilocybin, and 155 received a placebo. In nine of these studies, therapy was provided alongside psilocybin administration. Collectively, the research indicated that psilocybin, particularly when paired with psychotherapy, yields beneficial outcomes with few serious side effects. The drug produced both rapid and lasting improvements after just one to three doses. Nonetheless, the authors emphasise the need for larger, double-blind trials with long-term objective measures before psilocybin can be adopted in routine clinical practice.

Despite encouraging evidence for psilocybin-assisted psychotherapy (PAP) in treating depression, standardisation of psychotherapeutic protocols remains a critical gap in clinical research. Chisamore et al. (2024) highlight that while PAP shows promise as a treatment for depression, supported by RCTs demonstrating preliminary safety and efficacy, there is a notable lack of uniformity across therapeutic methods. Their review aimed to summarise and compare existing psychotherapeutic protocols used in clinical trials targeting depression and psychological distress related to life-threatening illnesses. The researchers systematically searched four

G. Bennett, *Psilocybin Therapy*, SpringerBriefs in Modern Perspectives on Disability Research, https://doi.org/10.1007/978-981-95-4119-5_2

databases—Embase, MEDLINE, PsycINFO, and CINAHL—and, after a multi-stage screening process, included 28 studies in their final analysis. They found that although all protocols incorporated preparatory sessions, monitored dosing, and post-session integration, considerable inconsistencies existed in other aspects, such as the structure, duration, and theoretical basis of the therapies. Furthermore, many studies failed to clearly articulate their therapeutic approaches. The authors conclude that while a foundational framework exists for PAP, the lack of detailed and standardised reporting hinders the development of a validated, widely accepted therapeutic protocol. They recommend that research in the future should focus more on clearly defining and documenting the psychotherapeutic components to establish safe and effective practices for PAP.

Psilocybin-based therapies are emerging as a promising alternative for managing depression, offering rapid and lasting benefits with minimal dosing. Dawood Hristova and Pérez-Jover (2023) note that depression remains a widespread mental health condition, affecting 280 million people globally and contributing significantly to disability and mortality. Psychedelic treatments—particularly those using psilocybin—have shown considerable promise as therapeutic options for depression. Reported benefits include swift and substantial reductions in depressive symptoms, enhanced well-being lasting for months post-treatment, and greater self-reflective insight. Their study aimed to generate experimental evidence on how psilocybin can be used therapeutically to treat major depressive disorder (MDD). It reviewed eight studies, some focused on treatment-resistant forms of depression while others focused on depression linked to severe, life-threatening illnesses such as cancer (see Appendix 2). Across these studies, psilocybin therapy—administered in just one or two sessions and accompanied by psychological support—consistently demonstrated its effectiveness in alleviating depressive symptoms. They concluded that:

> Psilocybin treatment for depression represents a promising paradigm for the fields of psychology and psychiatry. The growing number of experimental studies that demonstrate the efficiency of this substance highlights its therapeutic potential and minimizes adverse effects. Therefore, even though psilocybin is still classified as a harmful substance due to its legal and cultural history it could lead to a positive revolution in this field and become a novel antidepressant intervention. By carrying out a procedurally appropriate and adaptive use, it could significantly expand the range of possible medical applications, such as depression, post-traumatic stress disorder, addictions, and obsessive-compulsive disorder. (Dawood Hristova & Pérez-Jover, 2023, pp. 12–13).

Recent meta-analytic evidence supports psilocybin's strong antidepressant effects, although further research is needed to clarify its long-term safety and optimal use. Fang et al. (2024) explored the effectiveness, tolerability, and overall suitability of psilocybin as a treatment for both primary depression—such as MDD—and secondary depression arising from serious health conditions or terminal diagnoses. Drawing on data from clinical trials sourced from PubMed, EMBASE, Web of Science, the Cochrane Library, and ClinicalTrials.gov (updated to 4 October 2023), they conducted a systematic review and meta-analysis. Of the 10 studies identified, eight were included in the meta-analysis, encompassing 524 adult participants. The results indicated a substantial antidepressant effect in favour of psilocybin, with a large effect size (Hedges' g = -0.89), though there was notable heterogeneity across studies (I^2 = 70.19%). Findings also suggested that larger doses were associated with stronger therapeutic outcomes. While most adverse effects were temporary and reversible, serious side effects were possible. The authors conclude that psilocybin appeared to offer both immediate and sustained relief from depressive symptoms, warranting its consideration as a complementary or alternative therapeutic option, though more research is needed to fully understand its risks and long-term benefits. They concluded that:

> our meta-analysis demonstrates the potential of psilocybin for providing short- and long-term relief from depression, with higher doses of psilocybin exhibiting stronger antidepressant effects. It is important to note that while few studies have reported serious adverse events following psilocybin use, these events cannot be disregarded. Further high-quality randomized controlled trials are necessary to investigate the efficacy of psilocybin in treating depression, particularly in patients with treatment-resistant depression. Additionally, future clinical studies should elucidate the relationship between dosage of psilocybin and both its antidepressant efficacy and adverse effects in order to determine the optimal therapeutic dose for depression treatment. (Fang et al., 2024, p. 12).

Meta-analytic findings suggest that PAP significantly reduces depressive symptoms, though further refinement of dosing strategies and trial designs is needed. Haikazian et al. (2023) conducted a systematic review and meta-analysis to assess the impact of psilocybin on depressive symptoms in individuals with either MDD or depression linked to life-threatening conditions. Their review incorporated data from randomised clinical trials and open-label studies, using a random-effects model to analyse the standardised mean difference (SMD) in depression scores from baseline to the primary endpoint, comparing psilocybin-treated groups to control groups. Out of 1734 initially identified studies, 13 (involving 686 participants) were included in their qualitative and/or quantitative synthesis. The meta-analysis of nine studies (n = 596) revealed a substantial antidepressant effect in favour of psilocybin (SMD = –0.78; $p < 0.001$), with high response and remission rates relative to controls. Open-label trials also consistently demonstrated marked reductions in depressive symptoms following psilocybin therapy. Psilocybin was generally well tolerated, with rare occurrences of serious adverse effects, such as suicidal ideation or behaviour, limited to individuals with pre-existing histories. Despite the encouraging results, the authors emphasise the need for more rigorous phase III trials to confirm efficacy, refine dosing protocols, and address challenges like functional unblinding by incorporating active placebos.

Li et al. (2022) aimed to assess how different doses of psilocybin influence its antidepressant effectiveness in treating primary depression and depression secondary to cancer. Using Preferred Reporting Items for Systematic Reviews and Meta-Analyses (PRISMA) guidelines, they systematically searched six databases for relevant studies published or ongoing up to 30 November 2020, including only those in English or Chinese. Seven studies involving 136 participants met their inclusion criteria. The analysis focused on changes in Beck Depression Inventory scores, with effect sizes measured by Hedges' g. Their results showed a strong overall antidepressant effect (Hedges' $g = 1.289$) with moderate heterogeneity. The antidepressant response followed a nonlinear pattern where efficacy initially declined but then improved as doses increased, with the optimal therapeutic effect occurring between 30–35 mg per 70 kg of body weight. Subgroup analyses highlighted that higher doses (30–35 mg/70 kg) yielded highly significant antidepressant benefits, effects were sustained for over a month, and primary depression patients responded particularly well. However, the authors caution that the limited number and varying quality of studies mean that their findings are preliminary. They recommend further clinical trials to confirm the optimal dosing and effectiveness of psilocybin.

Recent RCTs provide evidence that psilocybin can improve depressive and anxiety symptoms in MDD, though further large-scale studies are needed to confirm its long-term safety and effectiveness. Li et al. (2024) conducted a systematic review of RCTs to assess the efficacy, safety, and tolerability of psilocybin in adults diagnosed with MDD. Their literature search, updated until September 14, 2023, identified five RCTs involving 472 participants—274 receiving psilocybin and 198 in control groups. Among these studies, three reported positive effects of psilocybin on depression symptoms, while two showed mixed results. Additionally, four RCTs demonstrated that psilocybin significantly improved anxiety symptoms compared to controls. Improvements in suicidal ideation were observed in one study. Rates of study discontinuation were similar between psilocybin and control groups. Adverse drug reactions were mostly mild, with headaches being the most frequently reported side effect (see Appendix 3). The authors conclude that psilocybin shows promise for alleviating depressive and anxiety symptoms in MDD, but emphasise the need for larger trials to establish its long-term safety and efficacy.

Meta-analytic evidence indicates that psilocybin-assisted therapy provides moderate to strong antidepressant benefits for MDD, though it carries a modestly increased risk of mild adverse effects. Menon et al. (2024) reviewed RCTs to evaluate the effectiveness and safety of psychedelic-assisted therapy, specifically psilocybin, in treating MDD, including treatment-resistant cases. They searched multiple databases up to April 2024 and identified six eligible RCTs involving 427 participants. The primary measure was the change in depression severity at approximately one-week post-treatment, with secondary assessments at days 2, 14, and 42. Results showed that psilocybin-assisted therapy significantly reduced depressive symptoms compared to control treatments, with a standardised mean difference of −0.72 at one week and consistent effects at other time points. The therapy also greatly increased the likelihood of clinical response and remission, with risk ratios over three for both outcomes. However, patients receiving psilocybin had a slightly higher chance of experiencing any adverse event, particularly headaches and dizziness. Most analyses showed low variability, and sensitivity checks supported these findings. The authors conclude that psilocybin-assisted therapy offers superior antidepressant effects lasting at least six weeks, accompanied by manageable side effects.

Psilocybin demonstrates significant antidepressant effects, especially in secondary depression and among individuals with prior psychedelic experience, though further research is needed to clarify moderating factors. Metaxa and Clarke (2024) conducted a systematic review and meta-analysis to evaluate psilocybin's effectiveness as an antidepressant compared to placebo or non-psychoactive drugs. They searched a wide range of published and unpublished literature databases and included randomised trials where psilocybin was given as a standalone treatment to adults with clinically significant depression symptoms. The analysis involved 436 participants, averaging 36 to 60 years of age, drawn from seven eligible studies. Results showed a moderate and statistically significant benefit of psilocybin on reducing depression scores (Hedges' $g = 0.66$). Subgroup analyses revealed larger treatment effects for patients with secondary depression (such as depression linked to medical conditions), when self-report scales like the Beck Depression Inventory were used, and among participants who were older or had previously used psychedelics. Although the studies had a moderate risk of bias, the overall quality of evidence was moderate, with low heterogeneity and little indication of publication bias. The authors recommend further research to better understand how factors such as expectancy effects, patient characteristics, and treatment methods influence psilocybin's antidepressant efficacy.

A dose-response meta-analysis identifies optimal psilocybin dosages for treating different types of depression, highlighting the need to balance efficacy with side effects. Perez et al. (2023) conducted a systematic review and dose-response meta-analysis to determine the most effective psilocybin doses for reducing depressive symptoms in adults with primary or secondary depression. Following a registered protocol, they searched multiple electronic databases up to February 2023, focusing on double-blind, randomised, placebo-controlled fixed-dose trials. Their analysis included seven studies with a total of 489 participants—366 with primary depression (including treatment-resistant cases) and 123 with secondary depression. The estimated effective doses to achieve 95% efficacy varied by group: 8.92 mg/70 kg for secondary depression, 24.68 mg/70 kg for primary depression, and 36.08 mg/70 kg when combining both groups. Dose-response curves showed significant associations, with most levelling off except for a bell-shaped curve in secondary depression. The study also revealed dose-related increases in side effects like physical discomfort, elevated blood pressure, nausea, headaches, and risk of prolonged psychosis. The authors conclude that more RCTs are necessary to refine optimal dosing for different patient groups, maximising therapeutic benefits while minimising adverse effects. They concluded that:

> our findings suggest a dose-response relationship for the use of psilocybin combined with psychotherapeutic support in treating primary depression, with a curve that reaches a plateau. The optimal therapeutic dose, beyond which no further therapeutic gain is observed, depends on the specific patient population and potential confounding factors like age and previous psychedelic experience. In the short term and in clinical settings, psilocybin demonstrates a reasonable safety profile with transient and mostly benign adverse events. This dose-response curve for the efficacy of psilocybin will aid in designing future clinical trials, particularly for populations with treatment-resistant depression and other co-morbid diagnoses related to depression. (Perez et al., 2023, p. 73).

Psilocybin shows rapid and lasting antidepressant effects, especially for treatment-resistant depression, but further rigorous research is needed to clarify its mechanisms and comparative efficacy. Prouzeau et al. (2022) reviewed the current evidence regarding the use of psilocybin in treating depression, emphasising both its clinical effectiveness and underlying mechanisms. The findings indicate that psilocybin produces a strong, fast-acting, and sustained antidepressant effect, particularly in cases of treatment-resistant or end-of-life depression. Patients generally tolerate psilocybin well, with side effects being mild and short-lived. However, existing studies have been limited by small sample sizes. Notably, one clinical trial comparing psilocybin to the antidepressant escitalopram did not find significant superiority for psilocybin in its primary outcome. The neurobiological processes involved in psilocybin's effects remain largely unknown but appear distinct from those of traditional SSRIs. The authors conclude that psilocybin is a promising alternative for depression treatment, but more extensive research, especially larger trials comparing it directly to established treatments, is essential to better understand its mechanisms and clinical potential.

Psilocybin shows promising rapid antidepressant effects, but further placebo-controlled trials are needed to confirm its long-term benefits and safety. Aghajanian et al. (2024) conducted a systematic review and meta-analysis to assess the effectiveness of psilocybin in treating depression, motivated by the limited success of current antidepressants. Psilocybin, a classic hallucinogen, is believed to alleviate depressive symptoms through its action on serotonergic and glutamatergic systems. The researchers performed an extensive search of PubMed and the Cochrane Library, selecting studies that examined psilocybin's therapeutic impact on depression. Using a mixed-effects multi-level model, they calculated the overall effect size and explored the treatment's effectiveness over time. Their findings support psilocybin's ability to significantly reduce depressive symptoms, with noticeable improvements observed as early as two weeks post-treatment. These acute remission effects highlight psilocybin's potential as a rapid-acting antidepressant. Although the review incorporates recent studies and employs rigorous methods, the authors emphasise the need for further well-controlled placebo trials to determine psilocybin's long-term efficacy and advantages over existing therapies. They conclude that advancing the use of psychedelics in depression treatment requires careful balancing of benefits, risks, and underlying mechanisms.

Recent evidence suggests that both single- and two-dose psilocybin treatments significantly reduce depressive symptoms in MDD and treatment-resistant depression, though more standardised research is needed to clarify dosing effects. Salvetti et al. (2024) highlight that existing pharmacological treatments for MDD often have limited effectiveness, with many patients developing treatment-resistant depression. Psilocybin, a classic serotonergic psychedelic, has gained attention as a promising treatment for these conditions. This systematic review and meta-analysis aimed to summarise recent findings on the impact of single and two-dose psilocybin administrations on depression severity, and to compare their efficacy in patients diagnosed with primary MDD or treatment-resistant depression. Following the PRISMA guidelines, the authors searched EBSCOhost and PubMed, initially identifying 425 articles, with 12 studies meeting inclusion criteria after screening. Their quantitative analysis showed that psilocybin effectively reduces depressive symptoms in both patient groups. While both dosing strategies demonstrated significant symptom reduction, two-dose treatments sometimes produced stronger and longer-lasting effects (see Appendix 4). However, it remains uncertain whether these differences stem from dosage alone or other factors. The authors recommend future standardised trials directly comparing these dosing regimens to better guide clinical use. They concluded that:

> The results from the clinical trials analyzed in this systematic review and meta-analysis underline the efficacy of psilocybin in the treatment of MDD patients, identifying this psychedelic tryptamine as a possible tool for the treatment of such disorders. Indeed, comparing the effects of a single and two-dose psilocybin administration, both treatment strategies were associated with a significant decrease in depressive symptoms severity compared to baseline assessment. Nonetheless, subsequent clinical trials, systematic reviews, and meta-analyses aimed at furthering this research topic are essential. With the results provided by future investigations, it could be possible to elaborate a more in-depth analysis of the available efficacy data, thus favoring the construction of evidence-based guidelines for intervention that would make the use of psilocybin within clinical settings more feasible and reliable. (Salvetti et al., 2024, p. 14).

Psilocybin shows significant promise as a safer and effective alternative to SSRIs for treating MDD, but standardised treatment protocols and further research are needed. Watford and Masood (2024) review the limited but growing body of research on psilocybin, a classical psychedelic historically used for healing but restricted in modern times due to its Schedule I classification. Despite regulatory challenges and few FDA-approved studies, increasing evidence highlights psilocybin's antidepressant effects, primarily through its action on 5-HT1a receptors, particularly in MDD. Their systematic review analysed six studies involving 319 participants, evenly split between RCTs and open-label studies. Psychological support was a consistent component across all treatments. Each study reported significant reductions in depressive symptoms with psilocybin, accompanied by relatively few side effects, positioning psilocybin favourably compared to traditional SSRIs, which often carry higher risks and adverse effects. The authors argue that psilocybin holds potential as a clinical treatment for depression but emphasise the need for future research to establish standardised treatment protocols, including session timing and types of psychological support. Additionally, more clinical trials are necessary to confirm efficacy and rule out publication bias. With these developments, psilocybin could revolutionise depression treatment and offer an alternative to existing antidepressants.

Clinical trials demonstrate that psilocybin produces rapid and sustained antidepressant and anxiolytic effects, particularly in treatment-resistant depression and cancer-related distress, with ongoing research needed to optimise dosing and assess long-term safety. Wang et al. (2024) reviewed the growing evidence for psilocybin's therapeutic potential in depression, highlighting its FDA breakthrough therapy designation for treatment-resistant depression in 2018. Psilocybin acts as a 5-HT2A receptor agonist, producing antidepressant and anxiolytic effects by enhancing glutamate transmission, reducing brain inflammation, and decreasing activity in the brain's default mode network. The authors identified eleven clinical trials investigating psilocybin's effects: six open-label studies and five double-blind randomised controlled trials (DB-RCTs). Open-label studies, including a pilot trial with treatment-resistant depression patients, reported significant symptom reductions after two psilocybin sessions and improvements in cognitive biases linked to depression. Follow-up studies confirmed sustained symptom improvement and high remission rates. Among DB-RCTs, two trials found that psilocybin significantly reduced anxiety and depression in cancer patients, with effects lasting over six months. In MDD, psilocybin produced rapid symptom relief and higher remission rates than escitalopram in one DB-RCT. Another DB-RCT demonstrated greater depression reduction within six hours post-dose compared to placebo. Additionally, in treatment-resistant depression, a 25 mg dose of psilocybin was more effective than 10 mg or 1 mg doses. Overall, psilocybin shows promising antidepressant and anxiolytic properties with a favourable safety profile, though further research is needed to determine optimal dosing and long-term outcomes. They concluded that:

> when used as an adjunctive therapy in psychiatric treatment, psilocybin shows a high potential for antidepressant effects, and these effects can persist over an extended period. Furthermore, there is research indicating its effectiveness in improving depression, anxiety, and quality of life in terminally ill cancer patients when used appropriately. Therefore, when used correctly, psilocybin is expected to have high clinical utility. Finally, as there have been cases of misuse in the past in the United States, appropriate regulation, and a high level of responsibility from expert groups are deemed necessary. (Wang et al., 2024, p. 230).

2.2 Conclusion

The growing body of research underscores psilocybin's considerable antidepressant and anxiolytic benefits, demonstrating both rapid onset and durable effects across diverse patient populations, including those with treatment-resistant depression and cancer-related psychological distress. Meta-analytic findings affirm moderate to large effect sizes, though variability across studies calls for more precise dosing guidelines and standardised therapy frameworks. While psilocybin's safety profile appears favourable compared to conventional antidepressants, vigilance regarding adverse events remains essential. The evidence collectively advocates for expanded, methodologically rigorous trials that can address current limitations, clarify mechanisms of action, and support the development of validated treatment protocols. As the field advances, psilocybin holds promise to become an important alternative or adjunct in depression management, potentially transforming therapeutic approaches within psychiatry.

References

Aghajanian, S., Shafiee, A., Parvizi Omran, S., Rezaei Nejad, A., Jafarabady, K., Kohandel Gargari, O., Rajai, S., Mohammadi, I., Bahrami Babaheidari, T., & Bakhtiyari, M. (2024). Psilocybin for major depressive disorder: An updated systematic review and meta-analysis of randomized clinical trials. *Journal of Psychopharmacology (Oxford, England)*, 2698811241287542. Advance online publication. https://doi.org/10.1177/02698811241287542

Chisamore, N., Johnson, D., Chen, M. J. Q., Offman, H., Chen-Li, D., Kaczmarek, E. S., Doyle, Z., McIntyre, R. S., & Rosenblat, J. D. (2024). Protocols and practices in psilocybin assisted psychotherapy for depression: A systematic review. *Journal of Psychiatric Research, 176*, 77–84. https://doi.org/10.1016/j.jpsychires.2024.05.051

Dawood Hristova, J. J., & Pérez-Jover, V. (2023). Psychotherapy with psilocybin for depression: Systematic review. *Behavioral sciences (Basel, Switzerland), 13*(4), 297. https://doi.org/10.3390/bs13040297

Fang, S., Yang, X., & Zhang, W. (2024). Efficacy and acceptability of psilocybin for primary or secondary depression: A systematic review and meta-analysis of randomized controlled trials. *Frontiers in Psychiatry, 15*, 1359088. https://doi.org/10.3389/fpsyt.2024.1359088

Haikazian, S., Chen-Li, D. C. J., Johnson, D. E., Fancy, F., Levinta, A., Husain, M. I., Mansur, R. B., McIntyre, R. S., & Rosenblat, J. D. (2023). Psilocybin-assisted therapy for depression: A systematic review and meta-analysis. *Psychiatry Research, 329*, 115531. https://doi.org/10.1016/j.psychres.2023.115531

Li, L. J., Mo, Y., Shi, Z. M., Huang, X. B., Ning, Y. P., Wu, H. W., Yang, X. H., & Zheng, W. (2024). Psilocybin for major depressive disorder: A systematic review of randomized controlled studies. *Frontiers in Psychiatry, 15*, 1416420. https://doi.org/10.3389/fpsyt.2024.1416420

Li, N. X., Hu, Y. R., Chen, W. N., & Zhang, B. (2022). Dose effect of psilocybin on primary and secondary depression: A preliminary systematic review and meta-analysis. *Journal of Affective Disorders, 296*, 26–34. https://doi.org/10.1016/j.jad.2021.09.041

Menon, V., Ramamurthy, P., Venu, S., & Andrade, C. (2025). Randomized Controlled Trials of Psilocybin-Assisted Therapy in the Treatment of Major Depressive Disorder: Systematic Review and Meta-Analysis. *Acta psychiatrica Scandinavica, 151*(5), 557–571. https://doi.org/10.1111/acps.13778

Metaxa, A. M., & Clarke, M. (2024). Efficacy of psilocybin for treating symptoms of depression: Systematic review and meta-analysis. *BMJ (Clinical Research Ed.), 385*, e078084. https://doi.org/10.1136/bmj-2023-078084

Perez, N., Langlest, F., Mallet, L., De Pieri, M., Sentissi, O., Thorens, G., Seragnoli, F., Zullino, D., Kirschner, M., Kaiser, S., Solmi, M., & Sabé, M. (2023). Psilocybin-assisted therapy for depression: A systematic review and dose-response meta-analysis of human studies. *European Neuropsychopharmacology: The Journal of the European College of Neuropsychopharmacology, 76*, 61–76. https://doi.org/10.1016/j.euroneuro.2023.07.011

Prouzeau, D., Conejero, I., Voyvodic, P. L., Becamel, C., Abbar, M., & Lopez-Castroman, J. (2022). Psilocybin efficacy and mechanisms of action in major depressive disorder: A review. *Current Psychiatry Reports, 24*(10), 573–581. https://doi.org/10.1007/s11920-022-01361-0

Salvetti, G., Saccenti, D., Moro, A. S., Lamanna, J., & Ferro, M. (2024). Comparison between single-dose and two-dose psilocybin administration in the treatment of major depression: A systematic review and meta-analysis of current clinical trials. *Brain Sciences, 14*(8), 829. https://doi.org/10.3390/brainsci14080829

van Amsterdam, J., & van den Brink, W. (2022). The therapeutic potential of psilocybin: A systematic review. *Expert Opinion on Drug Safety, 21*(6), 833–840. https://doi.org/10.1080/14740338.2022.2047929

Wang, S. M., Kim, S., Choi, W. S., Lim, H. K., Woo, Y. S., Pae, C. U., & Bahk, W. M. (2024). Current understanding on psilocybin for major depressive disorder: A review focusing on clinical trials. *Clinical Psychopharmacology and Neuroscience: The Official Scientific Journal of the Korean College of Neuropsychopharmacology, 22*(2), 222–231. https://doi.org/10.9758/cpn.23.1134

Watford, T., & Masood, N. (2024). Psilocybin, an effective treatment for major depressive disorder in adults - A systematic review. *Clinical Psychopharmacology and Neuroscience: The Official Scientific Journal of the Korean College of Neuropsychopharmacology, 22*(1), 2–12. https://doi.org/10.9758/cpn.23.1120

Additional Readings

Aday, J. S., Mitzkovitz, C. M., Bloesch, E. K., Davoli, C. C., & Davis, A. K. (2020). Long-term effects of psychedelic drugs: A systematic review. *Neuroscience and Biobehavioral Reviews, 113*, 179–189. https://doi.org/10.1016/j.neubiorev.2020.03.017

This systematic review synthesises findings from 34 experimental studies examining the long-term psychological and behavioural effects of classic psychedelics in human subjects, with follow-up periods of at least two weeks. Psilocybin was the most commonly studied substance. The review identifies lasting changes across domains such as personality, mood, mindfulness, and substance use. Key mediators of these effects included mystical experiences and emotional breakthroughs. Adverse effects were minimal when appropriate safeguards were in place. The authors call for future research with more diverse samples, longer follow-up durations, and improved methodological consistency. This work highlights the therapeutic promise of psychedelics while emphasising the need for rigorous long-term evaluations.

Romeo, B., Kervadec, E., Fauvel, B., Strika-Bruneau, L., Amirouche, A., Verroust, V., Piolino, P., & Benyamina, A. (2024). Safety and risk assessment of psychedelic psychotherapy: A meta-analysis and systematic review. *Psychiatry Research, 335*, 115880. https://doi.org/10.1016/j.psychres.2024.115880

This meta-analysis and systematic review evaluates the safety profile of psychedelic-assisted psychotherapy in over 1,000 administrations across 30 studies. The analysis focused on both acute and subacute adverse effects, including cardiovascular responses and psychiatric risks. Serious adverse events were rare, with only nine cases reported, and no suicide attempts occurred during the acute phase. The most common side effects included increased heart rate and blood pressure, nausea, headaches, and transient anxiety. The authors conclude that psychedelics are generally well-tolerated in controlled clinical settings with appropriate screening procedures. This study provides critical safety data to support ongoing clinical use and future regulatory evaluations.

Yao, Y., Guo, D., Lu, T. S., Liu, F. L., Huang, S. H., Diao, M. Q., Li, S. X., Zhang, X. J., Kosten, T. R., Shi, J., Bao, Y. P., Lu, L., & Han, Y. (2024). Efficacy and safety of psychedelics for the treatment of mental disorders: A systematic review and meta-analysis. *Psychiatry Research, 335*, 115886. https://doi.org/10.1016/j.psychres.2024.115886

This large-scale systematic review and meta-analysis synthesises data from 126 studies on the efficacy and safety of psychedelics—particularly psilocybin, ayahuasca, LSD, and MDMA—in treating various mental disorders. Psilocybin had the strongest therapeutic effect, particularly for mood disorders, followed by ayahuasca, MDMA, and LSD. The review also found limited but promising evidence for psychedelic-assisted treatment of conditions like tobacco addiction, sleep disorders, and OCD. Headaches were the most commonly reported adverse event, though nearly a third of studies reported no lasting side effects. The findings support the potential of psychedelics to alleviate symptoms across a range of psychiatric conditions, while highlighting the need for further research into long-term safety and efficacy.

Yerubandi, A., Thomas, J. E., Bhuiya, N. M. M. A., Harrington, C., Villa Zapata, L., & Caballero, J. (2024). Acute adverse effects of therapeutic doses of psilocybin: A systematic review and meta-analysis. *JAMA Network Open, 7*(4), e245960. https://doi.org/10.1001/jamanetworkopen.2024.5960

This systematic review and meta-analysis focuses specifically on the acute adverse effects of psilocybin at therapeutic doses in clinical trials targeting depression and anxiety. Drawing from six randomised, double-blind trials involving 528 participants, the study identifies significant short-term side effects including headache, nausea, anxiety, dizziness, and elevated blood pressure. These effects typically resolved within 48 hours. Notably, psilocybin was not associated with increased risk of paranoia or transient thought disorder. The study underscores psilocybin's generally tolerable safety profile in therapeutic contexts, while emphasising the importance of monitoring and managing short-term physiological and psychological effects in clinical practice.

Yildirim, B., Sahin, S. S., Gee, A., Jauhar, S., Rucker, J., Salgado-Pineda, P., Pomarol-Clotet, E., & McKenna, P. (2024). Adverse psychiatric effects of psychedelic drugs: A systematic review of case reports. *Psychological Medicine, 54*(15), 1–13. Advance online publication. https://doi.org/10.1017/S0033291724002496

This systematic review compiles case reports documenting psychiatric adverse effects following psychedelic drug use, with a focus on schizophrenia spectrum disorders, affective disorders, and flashbacks. After excluding cases involving other drug use or prior psychiatric history, the review identifies 17 cases each of schizophrenia and affective disorders, often triggered by a single psychedelic experience. Flashbacks with persistent psychiatric symptoms were also reported, though many resolved within a year. While such outcomes appear rare, the study highlights that serious psychiatric events can occur in vulnerable individuals. It contributes to the risk assessment literature by emphasising the importance of rigorous screening in psychedelic therapy protocols.

Chapter 3
Current Research Limitations and Opportunities for Studying Psilocybin's Therapeutic Benefits in Treating Depression

3.1 Design Limitations in the Studies Reviewed

3.1.1 Small Sample Sizes Limiting Generalisability and Statistical Power

Small sample sizes were commonly noted across multiple studies. This limitation constrains the statistical power of analyses, increasing the likelihood of both Type I and Type II errors. With fewer participants, variability within the population cannot be fully captured, weakening the ability to detect genuine treatment effects and diminishing the external validity of findings. For research in the future, larger, multisite randomised controlled trials are needed to ensure more robust and representative data. Funding bodies and collaborative research organisations should support recruitment across diverse populations to increase the scalability of results (see Table 3.1).

3.1.2 Heterogeneity in Study Designs, Dosing Regimens, Outcome Measures, and Populations

The variation in methodologies—including dosing protocols, sample characteristics, therapeutic support, and depression measurement tools—poses a significant obstacle to synthesising findings across studies. Such heterogeneity leads to inconsistent outcomes, inflated confidence intervals, and difficulties in drawing meaningful comparisons or performing meta-analyses. This variability undermines the development of standardised treatment guidelines. Future studies should prioritise harmonising key methodological elements and adhere to common reporting

G. Bennett, *Psilocybin Therapy*, SpringerBriefs in Modern Perspectives on Disability Research, https://doi.org/10.1007/978-981-95-4119-5_3

standards, such as the CONSORT guidelines, to improve comparability and data pooling across trials (see Table 3.1).

3.1.3 Lack of Standardisation and/or Inadequate Reporting of Psychotherapeutic Protocols

Many studies failed to describe their psychotherapeutic frameworks in sufficient detail or used varied therapeutic modalities without justification or transparency. This obscures the specific contribution of psychotherapy to treatment outcomes and complicates replication efforts. Furthermore, inadequate reporting limits the ability to identify best practices in psilocybin-assisted psychotherapy. To mitigate this issue, researchers should publish detailed therapy protocols and session structures, ideally including manuals or appendices, and distinguish the effects of drug administration from those of therapeutic interaction through careful study design (see Table 3.1).

3.1.4 Publication Bias and Limited Access to Unpublished or Incomplete Trial Data

The tendency for studies with positive results to be published more readily than those with negative or null findings distorts the perceived efficacy of psilocybin therapy. This bias inflates effect sizes in systematic reviews and meta-analyses, compromising the objectivity of evidence-based assessments. Moreover, incomplete trial data reduce the transparency and reproducibility of scientific findings. To address this, researchers should pre-register their trials on public platforms, publish all findings regardless of outcome, and share raw data when feasible to enable secondary analyses and verification (see Table 3.1).

3.1.5 Risk of Functional Unblinding and Expectancy Effects

Due to psilocybin's distinct psychoactive effects, participants and clinicians can often guess the treatment allocation, even in supposedly blinded studies. This "*functional unblinding*" introduces expectancy effects, where participants' beliefs about receiving an active substance influence reported outcomes. Such biases are especially problematic when using self-report measures. Researchers should design more effective blinding strategies—such as active placebos that mimic psychedelic effects—and assess expectancy prior to intervention. Collecting blinding integrity data is essential for interpreting the reliability of reported treatment effects (see Table 3.1).

3.1.6 Lack of Diversity in Participant Demographics (e.g., Ethnicity, Gender)

A consistent lack of racial, ethnic, and gender diversity among study participants limits the generalisability of findings to the broader population. Homogeneous samples fail to capture how demographic and sociocultural differences influence treatment outcomes, perpetuating inequities in research applicability. This limitation can be addressed by actively recruiting participants from underrepresented groups and designing studies with inclusive sampling frameworks. Reporting demographic breakdowns in publications should become standard practice, accompanied by subgroup analyses when appropriate (see Table 3.1).

3.1.7 Inadequate Control Groups or Lack of Active Comparators

Several trials lacked appropriate control conditions, such as placebo or active comparator groups, making it difficult to isolate the effects of psilocybin from other influences like the therapeutic setting. This undermines internal validity and limits the strength of causal inferences. Future studies should incorporate well-matched control groups, including active placebos or standard treatments, to facilitate direct comparison and strengthen conclusions about efficacy (see Table 3.1).

3.1.8 Confounding Effects of Psychological Support Not Controlled or Reported

Psychological support is often administered alongside psilocybin, but when its nature, intensity, or duration is poorly defined or uncontrolled, it becomes difficult to determine the independent effect of the drug. This conflation reduces the clarity of causal pathways and hinders reproducibility. To mitigate this, research in the future should clearly delineate the type of psychological support provided, control for therapist variables, and consider study designs that isolate pharmacological effects from psychotherapeutic contributions—such as crossover trials or dismantling studies (see Table 3.1).

3.1.9 Insufficient Data on Prior Psilocybin or Therapy Experience

Participant characteristics, including past use of psychedelics or prior therapy exposure, can substantially influence treatment responsiveness. Without this information, interpreting outcome variability becomes challenging, and subgroup effects may go unrecognised. Researchers should collect and report comprehensive baseline data, including prior psychedelic and psychological treatment history, and use stratified randomisation or covariate adjustment to control for these influences (see Table 3.1).

3.1.10 Use of Different Depression Assessment Tools with Varying Accuracy

The application of diverse depression scales—some clinician-administered and others self-reported—introduces variability in outcome measurement and reduces comparability between studies. Since different tools have differing sensitivity and specificity, their inconsistent use undermines the reliability of meta-analytic findings. Standardisation of depression measurement tools, prioritising those with strong psychometric properties, would enhance data quality and facilitate more accurate cross-study comparisons (see Table 3.1).

3.1.11 Inability to Isolate Psilocybin's Effect from Co-occurring Conditions (e.g., Cancer, Comorbidities)

Some studies included participants with serious comorbid conditions, such as cancer or anxiety disorders, which may affect both the manifestation of depression and the response to treatment. These uncontrolled variables introduce noise and complicate the attribution of outcomes solely to psilocybin. Future trials should either exclude participants with major confounding conditions or analyse subgroups separately to clarify differential effects (see Table 3.1).

3.1.12 Lack of Long-Term Follow-Up or Data on Sustained Effects and Safety

Short-term outcomes dominate the current literature, with few studies assessing whether benefits from psilocybin therapy persist beyond one or two months. This is a critical gap, as long-term efficacy and safety are essential for clinical translation. To address this, future research should incorporate extended follow-up periods and standardised safety monitoring, ideally over six months to a year, to determine the durability and risks of treatment effects (see Table 3.1).

3.1.13 Imprecise Methods Due to Data Imputation or Graphical Extraction

Some meta-analyses relied on extracted or imputed data, such as estimating standard deviations from figures, introducing potential inaccuracies into pooled estimates. These techniques, while sometimes necessary, can compromise the precision and reproducibility of findings. Researchers in the future should make raw data available and adhere to full reporting standards (e.g., Preferred Reporting Items for Systematic Reviews and Meta-Analyses (PRISMA)), while meta-analysts should note imputation limitations and prioritise studies with complete datasets for inclusion in primary analyses (see Table 3.1).

Table 3.1 Common limitations in the literature reviews examined for this book

Limitation Identified	References
Small sample sizes limiting generalisability and statistical power	Fang et al. (2024); Haikazian et al. (2023); Li et al. (2022); Li et al. (2024); Salvetti et al. (2024)
Heterogeneity in study designs, dosing regimens, outcome measures, and populations	Aghajanian et al. (2024); Fang et al. (2024); Haikazian et al. (2023); Li et al. (2022); Li et al. (2024); Perez et al. (2023); Salvetti et al. (2024)
Lack of standardisation and/or inadequate reporting of psychotherapeutic protocols	Aghajanian et al. (2024); Chisamore et al. (2024); Metaxa and Clarke (2024)
Publication bias and limited access to unpublished or incomplete trial data	Fang et al. (2024); Li et al. (2022); Perez et al. (2023)
Risk of functional unblinding and expectancy effects	Fang et al. (2024); Haikazian et al. (2023); Metaxa and Clarke (2024); Perez et al. (2023)
Lack of diversity in participant demographics (e.g., ethnicity, gender)	Haikazian et al. (2023); Metaxa and Clarke (2024); Salvetti et al. (2024)
Inadequate control groups or lack of active comparators	Haikazian et al. (2023); Li et al. (2022); Perez et al. (2023)
Confounding effects of psychological support not controlled or reported	Aghajanian et al. (2024); Li et al. (2024); Metaxa and Clarke (2024)
Insufficient data on prior psilocybin/therapy experience or participant characteristics	Metaxa and Clarke (2024); Salvetti et al. (2024)
Use of different depression assessment tools with varying accuracy	Aghajanian et al. (2024)
Inability to isolate psilocybin's effect from co-occurring conditions (e.g., cancer, comorbidities)	Li et al. (2022); Perez et al. (2023); Salvetti et al. (2024)
Lack of long-term follow-up or data on sustained effects and safety	Perez et al. (2023)
Imprecise methods due to data imputation or graphical extraction	Metaxa and Clarke (2024)

3.2 Opportunities to Study Psilocybin's Therapeutic Benefits in Treating Depression

Despite the amount of literature about psilocybin's therapeutic benefits in treating depression, there remains much research that needs to be conducted, especially if it can correct the shortcomings listed in Table 3.1. Prospective researchers can implement Salvetti et al.'s (2024) selection criteria to ensure that a systematic review is conducted to the best quality. According to Salvetti et al., to be included in a prospective systematic review, studies needed to meet the following inclusion criteria:

- *Language*: Only articles in English should be selected. This is for uniformity with other systematic reviews of the literature.
- *Population*: As it is the aim of a systematic literature review to investigate the efficacy of psilocybin with a focus on depression, it is considered necessary to select only the population with a primary diagnosis of depression, including subjects with treatment-resistant depression.
- *Types of studies*: Only data from clinical trials conducted on humans should be considered.
- *Intervention*: Only studies involving the administration of a single dose or two doses of psilocybin should be included, regardless of the specific dosage and mode of administration.
- *Outcome*: Only studies that assess a possible decrease in the severity of depressive symptoms among participants using standardised instruments should be included.

Conversely, according to Salvetti et al., studies should be excluded from a potential systematic review if:

- *Population*: Trials with participants who do not report a diagnosis of depression or report it as a secondary diagnosis to other psychiatric disorders.
- *Types of studies*: Clinical trials performed on animal models or case studies.
- *Intervention*: Studies in which other psychedelics than psilocybin, e.g., mescaline or bufotenine, are administered to patients, as well as studies involving no or more than two doses of psilocybin.
- *Outcome*: Trial studies that do not include scales measuring depressive symptoms or in which timepoints were missing were excluded.

3.3 Conclusion

Despite the excitement surrounding psilocybin therapy for treating depression, the field remains in a formative stage, with many studies constrained by methodological weaknesses that limit the strength of their conclusions. Recognising these limitations is essential not only for interpreting current findings with appropriate caution but also for guiding the development of more rigorous and inclusive research practices. Studies in the future must prioritise larger and more diverse samples, standardised methodologies, improved blinding procedures, and long-term follow-up to assess sustained outcomes. By addressing these concerns directly, researchers can generate more reliable and clinically actionable evidence, ultimately ensuring that psilocybin-based interventions are evaluated with the scientific integrity they require. This chapter serves as a foundation for advancing both the quality and credibility of psilocybin research as it transitions towards mainstream clinical application.

References

Aghajanian, S., Shafiee, A., Parvizi Omran, S., Rezaei Nejad, A., Jafarabady, K., Kohandel Gargari, O., Rajai, S., Mohammadi, I., Bahrami Babaheidari, T., & Bakhtiyari, M. (2024). Psilocybin for major depressive disorder: An updated systematic review and meta-analysis of randomized clinical trials. *Journal of Psychopharmacology (Oxford, England)*, 2698811241287542. Advance online publication. https://doi.org/10.1177/02698811241287542

Chisamore, N., Johnson, D., Chen, M. J. Q., Offman, H., Chen-Li, D., Kaczmarek, E. S., Doyle, Z., McIntyre, R. S., & Rosenblat, J. D. (2024). Protocols and practices in psilocybin assisted psychotherapy for depression: A systematic review. *Journal of Psychiatric Research, 176*, 77–84. https://doi.org/10.1016/j.jpsychires.2024.05.051

Fang, S., Yang, X., & Zhang, W. (2024). Efficacy and acceptability of psilocybin for primary or secondary depression: A systematic review and meta-analysis of randomized controlled trials. *Frontiers in Psychiatry, 15*, 1359088. https://doi.org/10.3389/fpsyt.2024.1359088

Haikazian, S., Chen-Li, D. C. J., Johnson, D. E., Fancy, F., Levinta, A., Husain, M. I., Mansur, R. B., McIntyre, R. S., & Rosenblat, J. D. (2023). Psilocybin-assisted therapy for depression: A systematic review and meta-analysis. *Psychiatry Research, 329*, 115531. https://doi.org/10.1016/j.psychres.2023.115531

Li, L. J., Mo, Y., Shi, Z. M., Huang, X. B., Ning, Y. P., Wu, H. W., Yang, X. H., & Zheng, W. (2024). Psilocybin for major depressive disorder: A systematic review of randomized controlled studies. *Frontiers in Psychiatry, 15*, 1416420. https://doi.org/10.3389/fpsyt.2024.1416420

Li, N. X., Hu, Y. R., Chen, W. N., & Zhang, B. (2022). Dose effect of psilocybin on primary and secondary depression: A preliminary systematic review and meta-analysis. *Journal of Affective Disorders, 296*, 26–34. https://doi.org/10.1016/j.jad.2021.09.041

Metaxa, A. M., & Clarke, M. (2024). Efficacy of psilocybin for treating symptoms of depression: Systematic review and meta-analysis. *BMJ (Clinical Research Ed.), 385*, e078084. https://doi.org/10.1136/bmj-2023-078084

Perez, N., Langlest, F., Mallet, L., De Pieri, M., Sentissi, O., Thorens, G., Seragnoli, F., Zullino, D., Kirschner, M., Kaiser, S., Solmi, M., & Sabé, M. (2023). Psilocybin-assisted therapy for depression: A systematic review and dose-response meta-analysis of human studies. *European Neuropsychopharmacology: The Journal of the European College of Neuropsychopharmacology, 76*, 61–76. https://doi.org/10.1016/j.euroneuro.2023.07.011

Salvetti, G., Saccenti, D., Moro, A. S., Lamanna, J., & Ferro, M. (2024). Comparison between single-dose and two-dose psilocybin administration in the treatment of major depression: A systematic review and meta-analysis of current clinical trials. *Brain sciences, 14*(8), 829. https://doi.org/10.3390/brainsci14080829

Chapter 4
Conclusion

In recent years, the renewed scientific and clinical interest in psilocybin has marked a transformative period in psychiatric research, particularly in the domain of depression treatment. This book has endeavoured to critically examine and synthesise the paucity of literature about psilocybin's therapeutic potential by focusing on secondary analyses, such as systematic literature reviews, that collectively distil findings from a broad spectrum of primary studies. By adopting this approach, this book not only highlights overarching themes and patterns but also provides a rigorous appraisal of the strengths, limitations, and gaps that define the current evidence base. In this concluding chapter, we revisit the key topics explored in the preceding chapters, contextualise their significance within the broader psychiatric and neuroscientific fields, and articulate pathways for future research and clinical practice.

The first chapter presented the history of psilocybin, from its indigenous and ceremonial use to its criminalisation and scientific obscurity during much of the twentieth century. The contemporary revival, driven by advances in neuropharmacology and growing recognition of mental health burdens worldwide, reflects a paradigm shift. Regulatory approvals, including breakthrough therapy designations and novel pharmaceutical development, have underscored both the scientific and commercial momentum behind psychedelic research. Additionally, Chap. 1 situated psilocybin research within its economic and policy contexts, illustrating how governmental initiatives and funding priorities have catalysed investigations into its efficacy and safety. This chapter also detailed the research questions and methodological frameworks that guide the synthesis in the following sections, ensuring the work is anchored in robust scientific inquiry.

Chapter 2 synthesised findings from a range of meta-analyses and systematic reviews, documenting psilocybin's promising therapeutic profile in the treatment of depression, especially treatment-resistant depression. The evidence suggests that psilocybin, often administered in conjunction with psychotherapeutic support, produces rapid, substantial, and durable improvements in depressive symptoms. Unlike traditional antidepressants such as selective serotonin reuptake inhibitors, which

G. Bennett, *Psilocybin Therapy*, SpringerBriefs in Modern Perspectives on Disability Research, https://doi.org/10.1007/978-981-95-4119-5_4

may take weeks to manifest clinical effects and often produce significant side effects, psilocybin's therapeutic impact is notable for its speed and relative safety. This chapter also underscored the importance of "*set and setting*"—the psychological state of the individual and the environmental context of administration—as critical determinants of therapeutic outcomes. This holistic view of treatment highlights the need to integrate psychotherapeutic frameworks with pharmacological intervention to optimise benefits and minimise risks.

Chapter 3 took a critical lens to the methodological limitations pervasive in psilocybin research. Small sample sizes, heterogeneity of study designs, insufficient blinding, and inconsistent reporting of key variables collectively undermine the reproducibility and generalisability of findings. These challenges complicate the translation of promising preliminary data into clinically actionable treatment protocols. This chapter also highlighted underexplored areas such as the variability in participant preparation, integration therapies post-session, and differential responses based on demographic or clinical subgroups. Addressing these gaps requires rigorous, standardised research frameworks that can accommodate the complexities of psychedelic-assisted therapy without compromising scientific rigour. Chapter 3 proposed strategic pathways to mitigate these issues, including the adoption of larger, multisite trials, consensus-building around therapeutic protocols, and enhanced transparency in data sharing and outcome reporting. Such efforts are essential to move the field beyond promising anecdotal and preliminary data towards robust, evidence-based guidelines that clinicians and regulatory bodies can trust.

Synthesising insights from all chapters, it is evident that psilocybin therapy stands at a promising yet precarious crossroads. The rapid and profound antidepressant effects observed in many trials suggest that psilocybin could revolutionise psychiatric treatment paradigms, particularly for individuals who do not respond to conventional therapies. However, this excitement must be tempered with caution. The limited size and scope of many studies, combined with the challenges inherent to psychedelic research (e.g., difficulties with effective placebo control and managing expectancy effects), require that stakeholders approach clinical implementation prudently. Safety remains paramount, with psychological support and careful screening emerging as non-negotiable components of responsible treatment frameworks.

The therapeutic application of psilocybin represents a bold frontier in psychiatric medicine, offering hope for millions affected by depression and other mental health disorders. This book's critical synthesis provides a clear-eyed view of both the promise and the challenges inherent in this evolving field. By grounding excitement in scientific rigour and ethical responsibility, it aims to support a measured yet optimistic progression of psilocybin therapy.

As research continues to advance, collaboration among scientists, clinicians, policymakers, and communities will be vital to realising psilocybin's full potential. With continued investment in high-quality research and thoughtful clinical integration, psilocybin could emerge as a transformative tool in the fight against depression, reshaping mental health care for the better.

Appendix

G. Bennett, *Psilocybin Therapy*, SpringerBriefs in Modern Perspectives on Disability Research, https://doi.org/10.1007/978-981-95-4119-5

Appendix 1: Dataset

PubMed ID	First author	Article title	Citation	Was the article included?
37844352	Haikazian S	Psilocybin-assisted therapy for depression: A systematic review and meta-analysis	*Psychiatry Res*. 2023 Nov;329:115531. doi: 10.1016/j.psychres.2023.115531. Epub 2023 Oct 11.	Yes
37557019	Perez N	Psilocybin-assisted therapy for depression: A systematic review and dose-response meta-analysis of human studies	*Eur Neuropsychopharmacol*. 2023 Nov;76:61-76. doi: 10.1016/j.euroneuro.2023.07.011. Epub 2023 Aug 7.	Yes
38692686	Metaxa AM	Efficacy of psilocybin for treating symptoms of depression: Systematic review and meta-analysis	*BMJ*. 2024 May 1;385:e078084. doi: 10.1136/bmj-2023-078084.	Yes
36232748	Psiuk D	Esketamine and Psilocybin—The Comparison of Two Mind-Altering Agents in Depression Treatment: Systematic Review	*Int J Mol Sci*. 2022 Sep 28;23(19):11450. doi: 10.3390/ijms231911450.	No
35253070	Sarparast A	Drug-drug interactions between psychiatric medications and MDMA or psilocybin: A systematic review	*Psychopharmacology (Berl)*. 2022 Jun;239(6):1945-1976. doi: 10.1007/s00213-022-06083-y. Epub 2022 Mar 7.	No
38781672	Fang Q	Efficacy and safety of psilocybin on treatment-resistant depression: A systematic review and meta-analysis	*Psychiatry Res*. 2024 Jul;337:115960. doi: 10.1016/j.psychres.2024.115960. Epub 2024 May 22.	No
38598236	Yerubandi A	Acute adverse effects of therapeutic doses of psilocybin: A systematic review and meta-analysis	*JAMA Netw Open*. 2024 Apr 1;7(4):e245960. doi: 10.1001/jamanetworkopen.2024.5960.	No
36381758	Goel DB	Potential therapeutic effects of psilocybin: A systematic review	*Cureus*. 2022 Oct 12;14(10):e30214. doi: 10.7759/cureus.30214. eCollection 2022 Oct.	No

36846225	van der Meer PB	Therapeutic effect of psilocybin in addiction: A systematic review	*Front Psychiatry*. 2023 Feb 9;14:1134454. doi: 10.3389/fpsyt.2023.1134454. eCollection 2023.	No
37102811	Dawood Hristova JJ	Psychotherapy with psilocybin for depression: Systematic review	*Behav Sci (Basel)*. 2023 Mar 31;13(4):297. doi: 10.3390/bs13040297.	Yes
39168500	Hsu TW	Comparative oral monotherapy of psilocybin, lysergic acid diethylamide, 3,4-methylenedioxymethamphetamine, ayahuasca, and escitalopram for depressive symptoms: Systematic review and Bayesian network meta-analysis	*BMJ*. 2024 Aug 21;386:e078607. doi: 10.1136/bmj-2023-078607.	No
37650489	Sharma P	Psilocybin history, action and reaction: A narrative clinical review	*J Psychopharmacol*. 2023 Sep;37(9):849-865. doi: 10.1177/02698811231190858. Epub 2023 Aug 31.	No
35811423	Dodd S	Psilocybin in neuropsychiatry: A review of its pharmacology, safety, and efficacy	*CNS Spectr*. 2023 Aug;28(4):416-426. doi: 10.1017/S1092852922000888. Epub 2022 Jul 11.	No
37395359	Bonnieux JN	Psilocybin's effects on cognition and creativity: A scoping review	*J Psychopharmacol*. 2023 Jul;37(7):635-648. doi: 10.1177/02698811231179801. Epub 2023 Jul 3.	No
37303932	Fonseka LN	Therapeutic role of psilocybin and 3,4-methylenedioxymethamphetamine in trauma: A literature review	*World J Psychiatry*. 2023 May 19;13(5):182-190. doi: 10.5498/wjp.v13.i5.182. eCollection 2023 May 19.	No
34451890	Więckiewicz G	Lysergic acid diethylamide, psilocybin and dimethyltryptamine in depression treatment: A systematic review	*Pharmaceuticals (Basel)*. 2021 Aug 12;14(8):793. doi: 10.3390/ph14080793.	No
39106989	Jevotovsky DS	Psilocybin and chronic neuropathic pain: A systematic review	*Reg Anesth Pain Med*. 2024 Aug 8:rapm-2024-105532. doi: 10.1136/rapm-2024-105532. Online ahead of print.	No

(continued)

(continued)

38850581	Chisamore N	Protocols and practices in psilocybin assisted psychotherapy for depression: A systematic review	*J Psychiatr Res*. 2024 Aug;176:77-84. doi: 10.1016/j.jpsychires.2024.05.051. Epub 2024 May 31.	Yes
37902038	Kaminski D	The tolerability and safety of psilocybin in psychiatric and substance-dependence conditions: A systematic review	*Ann Pharmacother*. 2024 Aug;58(8):811-826. doi: 10.1177/10600280231205645. Epub 2023 Oct 30.	No
35953638	Prouzeau D	Psilocybin efficacy and mechanisms of action in major depressive disorder: A review	*Curr Psychiatry Rep*. 2022 Oct;24(10):573-581. doi: 10.1007/s11920-022-01361-0. Epub 2022 Aug 12.	Yes
34293927	Horton DM	Systematized review of psychotherapeutic components of psilocybin-assisted psychotherapy	*Am J Psychother*. 2021 Dec 1;74(4):140-149. doi: 10.1176/appi.psychotherapy.20200055. Epub 2021 Jul 23.	No
39135496	Madden K	Psilocybin for clinical indications: A scoping review	*J Psychopharmacol*. 2024 Oct;38(10):839-845. doi: 10.1177/02698811241269751. Epub 2024 Aug 13.	No
35285280	Kisely S	A systematic literature review and meta-analysis of the effect of psilocybin and methylenedioxymethamphetamine on mental, behavioural or developmental disorders	*Aust N Z J Psychiatry*. 2023 Mar;57(3):362-378. doi: 10.1177/00048674221083868. Epub 2022 Mar 12.	No
35225143	van Amsterdam J	The therapeutic potential of psilocybin: A systematic review	*Expert Opin Drug Saf*. 2022 Jun;21(6):833-840. doi: 10.1080/14740338.2022.2047929. Epub 2022 Mar 2.	Yes
34587546	Li NX	Dose effect of psilocybin on primary and secondary depression: A preliminary systematic review and meta-analysis	*J Affect Disord*. 2022 Jan 1;296:26-34. doi: 10.1016/j.jad.2021.09.041. Epub 2021 Sep 17.	Yes
39778644	Erkizia-Santamaría I	Clinical and preclinical evidence of psilocybin as antidepressant. A narrative review	*Prog Neuropsychopharmacol Biol Psychiatry*. 2025 Jan 10;136:111249. doi: 10.1016/j.pnpbp.2025.111249. Epub 2025 Jan 6.	No

38525640	Van Der Walt J	LSD and psilocybin for chronic nociplastic pain: A narrative review of the literature supporting the use of classic psychedelic agents in chronic pain	*S Afr Med J*. 2023 Nov 6;113(11):22-26. doi: 10.7196/SAMJ.2023.v113i11.814.	No
32648791	Reinert JP	Management of overdoses of salvia, kratom, and psilocybin mushrooms: A literature review	*Expert Rev Clin Pharmacol*. 2020 Aug;13(8):847-856. doi: 10.1080/17512433.2020.1794811. Epub 2020 Jul 25.	No
34619818	Yu CL	Psilocybin for end-of-life anxiety symptoms: A systematic review and meta-analysis	*Psychiatry Investig*. 2021 Oct;18(10):958-967. doi: 10.30773/pi.2021.0209. Epub 2021 Oct 8.	No
39282928	Savides IA	Less is more? A review of psilocybin microdosing	*J Psychopharmacol*. 2024 Oct;38(10):846-860. doi: 10.1177/02698811241278769. Epub 2024 Sep 16.	No
39480198	Aghajanian S	Psilocybin for major depressive disorder: An updated systematic review and meta-analysis of randomized clinical trials	*J Psychopharmacol*. 2024 Oct 31:2698811241287542. doi: 10.1177/02698811241287542. Online ahead of print.	Yes
39354706	Meshkat S	Impact of psilocybin on cognitive function: A systematic review	*Psychiatry Clin Neurosci*. 2024 Dec;78(12):744-764. doi: 10.1111/pcn.13741. Epub 2024 Oct 1.	No
40266291	Borgogna NC	Incremental efficacy systematic review and meta-analysis of psilocybin-for-depression RCTs	*Psychopharmacology (Berl)*. 2025 Apr 23. doi: 10.1007/s00213-025-06788-w. Online ahead of print.	No
38877715	Polito V	Is microdosing a placebo? A rapid review of low-dose LSD and psilocybin research	*J Psychopharmacol*. 2024 Aug;38(8):701-711. doi: 10.1177/02698811241254831. Epub 2024 Jun 14.	No

(continued)

(continued)

39376971	Li LJ	Psilocybin for major depressive disorder: A systematic review of randomized controlled studies	*Front Psychiatry*. 2024 Sep 23;15:1416420. doi: 10.3389/fpsyt.2024.1416420. eCollection 2024.	Yes
39168642	Kim A	Psilocybin-assisted psychotherapy for existential distress: Practical considerations for therapeutic application—a review	*Ann Palliat Med*. 2024 Nov;13(6):1490-1501. doi: 10.21037/apm-24-35. Epub 2024 Aug 16.	No
38244804	Wong S	A comparison between psilocybin and esketamine in treatment-resistant depression using number needed to treat (NNT): A systematic review	*J Affect Disord*. 2024 Apr 1;350:698-705. doi: 10.1016/j.jad.2024.01.142. Epub 2024 Jan 18.	No
35273885	Ziff S	Analysis of psilocybin-assisted therapy in medicine: A narrative review	*Cureus*. 2022 Feb 5;14(2):e21944. doi: 10.7759/cureus.21944. eCollection 2022 Feb.	No
35207210	Yu CL	Trajectory of antidepressant effects after single- or two-dose administration of psilocybin: A systematic review and multivariate meta-analysis	*J Clin Med*. 2022 Feb 11;11(4):938. doi: 10.3390/jcm11040938.	No
39257234	Thaoboonruang N	Pharmacokinetics of psilocybin, a tryptamine alkaloid in magic mushroom (Psilocybe cubensis): A systematic review	*J Psychoactive Drugs*. 2024 Sep 10:1-13. doi: 10.1080/02791072.2024.2399128. Online ahead of print.	No
40245969	Meshkat S	Efficacy and safety of psilocybin for the treatment of substance use disorders: A systematic review	*Neurosci Biobehav Rev*. 2025 Jun;173:106163. doi: 10.1016/j.neubiorev.2025.106163. Epub 2025 Apr 15.	No
40143157	Galdino TP	Extraction yields of psilocybin and psilocin: A short review of current methods and their implications	*Pharmaceuticals (Basel)*. 2025 Mar 7;18(3):380. doi: 10.3390/ph18030380.	No
38659049	Downey AE	Psilocybin therapy and anorexia nervosa: A narrative review of safety considerations for researchers and clinicians	*J Eat Disord*. 2024 Apr 24;12(1):49. doi: 10.1186/s40337-024-01005-z.	No
38570038	Le GH	Spectral signatures of psilocybin, lysergic acid diethylamide (LSD) and ketamine in healthy volunteers and persons with major depressive disorder and treatment-resistant depression: A systematic review	*J Affect Disord*. 2024 Jun 15;355:342-354. doi: 10.1016/j.jad.2024.03.165. Epub 2024 Apr 1.	No

No32296353	Heuschkel K	Depression, mindfulness, and psilocybin: Possible complementary effects of mindfulness meditation and psilocybin in the treatment of depression. A Review	*Front Psychiatry*. 2020 Mar 31;11:224. doi: 10.3389/fpsyt.2020.00224. eCollection 2020.	No
39141970	Yang X	Letter to editor regarding "Psilocybin-assisted therapy for depression: A systematic review and meta-analysis"	*Psychiatry Res*. 2024 Oct;340:116136. doi: 10.1016/j.psychres.2024.116136. Epub 2024 Aug 8.	No
28481178	Thomas K	Psilocybin-assisted therapy: A review of a novel treatment for psychiatric disorders	*J Psychoactive Drugs*. 2017 Nov-Dec;49(5):446-455. doi: 10.1080/02791072.2017.1320734. Epub 2017 May 8.	No
40058407	Modzelewski S	Side effects of microdosing lysergic acid diethylamide and psilocybin: A systematic review of potential physiological and psychiatric outcomes	*Neuropharmacology*. 2025 Jun 15;271:110402. doi: 10.1016/j.neuropharm.2025.110402. Epub 2025 Mar 7.	No
36097251	Pouyan N	A research domain criteria (RDoC)-guided dashboard to review psilocybin target domains: A systematic review	*CNS Drugs*. 2022 Oct;36(10):1031-1047. doi: 10.1007/s40263-022-00944-y. Epub 2022 Sep 12.	No
33884324	Castro Santos H	What is the clinical evidence on psilocybin for the treatment of psychiatric disorders? A systematic review	*Porto Biomed J*. 2021 Feb 11;6(1):e128. doi: 10.1097/j.pbj.0000000000000128. eCollection 2021 Jan-Feb.	No
38627070	Wang SM	Current understanding on psilocybin for major depressive disorder: A review focusing on clinical trials	*Clin Psychopharmacol Neurosci*. 2024 May 31;22(2):222-231. doi: 10.9758/cpn.23.1134. Epub 2023 Nov 30.	Yes
39071471	Bader H	Investigating the therapeutic efficacy of psilocybin in advanced cancer patients: A comprehensive review and meta-analysis	*World J Clin Oncol*. 2024 Jul 24;15(7):908-919. doi: 10.5306/wjco.v15.i7.908.	No

(continued)

(continued)

38842300	Ramos L	The effects of psilocybin on cognition and emotional processing in healthy adults and adults with depression: A systematic literature review	*J Clin Exp Neuropsychol*. 2024 Jul;46(5):393-421. doi: 10.1080/13803395.2024.2363343. Epub 2024 Jun 6.	No
39199520	Salvetti G	Comparison between single-dose and two-dose psilocybin administration in the treatment of major depression: A systematic review and meta-analysis of current clinical trials	*Brain Sci*. 2024 Aug 18;14(8):829. doi: 10.3390/brainsci14080829.	Yes
32899469	Vargas AS	Psilocybin as a new approach to treat depression and anxiety in the context of life-threatening diseases—A systematic review and meta-analysis of clinical trials	*Biomedicines*. 2020 Sep 5;8(9):331. doi: 10.3390/biomedicines8090331.	No
27354908	Dos Santos RG	Antidepressive, anxiolytic, and antiaddictive effects of ayahuasca, psilocybin and lysergic acid diethylamide (LSD): A systematic review of clinical trials published in the last 25 years	*Ther Adv Psychopharmacol*. 2016 Jun;6(3):193-213. doi: 10.1177/2045125316638008. Epub 2016 Mar 18.	No
35645354	Edinoff AN	Alternative options for complex, recurrent pain states using cannabinoids, psilocybin, and ketamine: A narrative review of clinical evidence	*Neurol Int*. 2022 May 18;14(2):423-436. doi: 10.3390/neurolint14020035.	No
40456393	Berkovitch L	Neurocognitive effects of psilocybin: A systematic and comprehensive review of neuroimaging studies in humans	*Neurosci Biobehav Rev*. 2025 Aug;175:106239. doi: 10.1016/j.neubiorev.2025.106239. Epub 2025 May 31.	No
39641126	Terao I	Comparative antidepressant effects and safety of intravenous racemic ketamine, psilocybin and theta burst stimulation for major depressive disorder: A systematic review and network meta-analyses of randomized controlled trials	*PCN Rep*. 2024 Dec 4;3(4):e70042. doi: 10.1002/pcn5.70042. eCollection 2024 Dec.	No
39670342	Freitas RR	The safety of psilocybin-assisted psychotherapy: A systematic review	*Aust N Z J Psychiatry*. 2025 Feb;59(2):128-151. doi: 10.1177/00048674241289024. Epub 2024 Dec 13.	No

38730654	Bellman V	Review of psilocybin use for depression among cancer patients after approval in Oregon	*Cancers (Basel)*. 2024 Apr 27;16(9):1702. doi: 10.3390/cancers16091702.	No
37523886	Simonsson O	Assessing the risk of symptom worsening in psilocybin-assisted therapy for depression: A systematic review and individual participant data meta-analysis	*Psychiatry Res*. 2023 Sep;327:115349. doi: 10.1016/j.psychres.2023.115349. Epub 2023 Jul 23.	No
35679988	Felsch CL	Don't be afraid, try to meditate- potential effects on neural activity and connectivity of psilocybin-assisted mindfulness-based intervention for social anxiety disorder: A systematic review	*Neurosci Biobehav Rev*. 2022 Aug;139:104724. doi: 10.1016/j.neubiorev.2022.104724. Epub 2022 Jun 6.	No
40284409	Meshkat S	Pharmacokinetics of psilocybin: A systematic review	*Pharmaceutics*. 2025 Mar 25;17(4):411. doi: 10.3390/pharmaceutics17040411.	No
38426002	Fang S	Efficacy and acceptability of psilocybin for primary or secondary depression: A systematic review and meta-analysis of randomized controlled trials	*Front Psychiatry*. 2024 Feb 15;15:1359088. doi: 10.3389/fpsyt.2024.1359088. eCollection 2024.	Yes
36646257	Pedicini M	Utility of preclinical models in the study of psilocybin—A comprehensive review	*Neurosci Biobehav Rev*. 2023 Mar;146:105046. doi: 10.1016/j.neubiorev.2023.105046. Epub 2023 Jan 13.	No
39812743	Otto ME	Clinical pharmacokinetics of psilocin after psilocybin administration: A systematic review and post-hoc analysis	*Clin Pharmacokinet*. 2025 Jan;64(1):53-66. doi: 10.1007/s40262-024-01454-4. Epub 2025 Jan 15.	No
37387703	IsHak WW	The impact of psilocybin on patients experiencing psychiatric symptoms: A systematic review of randomized clinical trials	*Innov Clin Neurosci*. 2023 Spring;20(4-6):39-48.	No
37385217	Lee HJ	Psilocybin's potential mechanisms in the treatment of depression: A systematic review	*J Psychoactive Drugs*. 2024 Jul-Aug;56(3):301-315. doi: 10.1080/02791072.2023.2223195. Epub 2023 Jun 29.	No

(continued)

(continued)

32931403	Varker T	Efficacy of psychoactive drugs for the treatment of posttraumatic stress disorder: A systematic review of MDMA, ketamine, LSD and psilocybin	*J Psychoactive Drugs*. 2021 Jan-Mar;53(1):85-95. doi: 10.1080/02791072.2020.1817639. Epub 2020 Sep 15.	No
39967455	Dave M	Anaesthetic implications of psilocybin and lysergic acid diethylamide: What is old is now new: A narrative review on psychedelics and anaesthesia	*Eur J Anaesthesiol*. 2025 May 1;42(5):430-434. doi: 10.1097/EJA.0000000000002138. Epub 2025 Feb 18.	No
39627679	Menon V	Randomized controlled trials of psilocybin-assisted therapy in the treatment of major depressive disorder: Systematic review and meta-analysis	*Acta Psychiatr Scand*. 2024 Dec 3. doi: 10.1111/acps.13778. Online ahead of print.	Yes
35225726	Hodge AT	The use of psilocybin in the treatment of psychiatric disorders with attention to relative safety profile: A systematic review	*J Psychoactive Drugs*. 2023 Jan-Mar;55(1):40-50. doi: 10.1080/02791072.2022.2044096. Epub 2022 Feb 28.	No
34482761	Lehto RH	The role of psilocybin-assisted psychotherapy to support patients with cancer: A critical scoping review of the research	*J Holist Nurs*. 2022 Sep;40(3):265-280. doi: 10.1177/08980101211039086. Epub 2021 Sep 6.	No
39788410	Constantino JL	Neurobiological mechanisms of antidepressant properties of psilocybin: A systematic review of blood biomarkers	*Prog Neuropsychopharmacol Biol Psychiatry*. 2025 Jan 10;136:111251. doi: 10.1016/j.pnpbp.2025.111251. Epub 2025 Jan 7.	No
39829391	Liebnau J	Catalyst for change: Psilocybin's antidepressant mechanisms—A systematic review	*J Psychopharmacol*. 2025 May;39(5):397-415. doi: 10.1177/02698811241312866. Epub 2025 Jan 20.	No

36604312	Baker KM	An integrative review of measures of spirituality in experimental studies of psilocybin in serious illness populations	*Am J Hosp Palliat Care*. 2023 Nov;40(11):1261-1270. doi: 10.1177/10499091221147700. Epub 2023 Jan 5.	No
39847068	Yousefi P	Acute effects of psilocybin on attention and executive functioning in healthy volunteers: A systematic review and multilevel meta-analysis	*Psychopharmacology (Berl)*. 2025 Jun;242(6):1171-1196. doi: 10.1007/s00213-024-06742-2. Epub 2025 Jan 23.	No
39731144	Koning E	Exploring the neurobiological correlates of psilocybin-assisted psychotherapy in eating disorders: A review of potential methodologies and implications for the psychedelic study design	*J Eat Disord*. 2024 Dec 27;12(1):214. doi: 10.1186/s40337-024-01185-8.	No
39357666	Ordovich-Clarkson RD	Comparing psilocybin to metformin as neuroprotective agents against Parkinson's dementia: A systematic review of evidence and efficacy	*Prog Neuropsychopharmacol Biol Psychiatry*. 2025 Jan 10;136:111155. doi: 10.1016/j.pnpbp.2024.111155. Epub 2024 Sep 30.	No
39787428	Manzano-Nunez R	Exploring psychedelics pharmacology: A scoping review charting the course of psilocybin pharmacokinetics	*Clin Neuropharmacol*. 2025 Jan-Feb 01;48(1):13-19. doi: 10.1097/WNF.0000000000000617.	No
38019032	Gattuso JJ	Psilocybin as a lead candidate molecule in preclinical therapeutic studies of psychiatric disorders: A systematic review	*J Neurochem*. 2024 Sep;168(9):1687-1720. doi: 10.1111/jnc.16017. Epub 2023 Nov 29.	No
40351554	Yaden DB	A field-wide review and analysis of study materials used in psilocybin trials: Assessment of two decades of research	*Psychedelic Med (New Rochelle)*. 2025 Feb 27;3(1):1-18. doi: 10.1089/psymed.2024.0019. eCollection 2025 Mar.	No
37126863	Koning E	Psilocybin-assisted psychotherapy as a potential treatment for eating disorders: A narrative review of preliminary evidence	*Trends Psychiatry Psychother*. 2024;46:e20220597. doi: 10.47626/2237-6089-2022-0597. Epub 2023 Jun 6.	No

(continued)

(continued)

40381005	Borgogna NC	Correction to: Incremental efficacy systematic review and meta-analysis of psilocybin-for-depression RCTs	*Psychopharmacology (Berl)*. 2025 May 17. doi: 10.1007/s00213-025-06818-7. Online ahead of print.	No
40259688	Lapid MI	Evaluating the effectiveness of psilocybin in alleviating distress among cancer patients: A systematic review	*Palliat Support Care*. 2025 Apr 22;23:e99. doi: 10.1017/S147895152500032X.	No
38704154		EXPRESSION OF CONCERN: Efficacy of psilocybin for treating symptoms of depression: Systematic review and meta-analysis	*BMJ*. 2024 May 4;385:q1025. doi: 10.1136/bmj.q1025.	No
38247407	Watford T	Psilocybin, an effective treatment for major depressive disorder in adults—A systematic review	*Clin Psychopharmacol Neurosci*. 2024 Feb 29;22(1):2-12. doi: 10.9758/cpn.23.1120. Epub 2023 Oct 16.	Yes
39982684	Otto ME	Correction: Clinical pharmacokinetics of psilocin after psilocybin administration: A systematic review and post-hoc analysis	*Clin Pharmacokinet*. 2025 Mar;64(3):465. doi: 10.1007/s40262-025-01487-3.	No
39929528		CORRECTION: Efficacy of psilocybin for treating symptoms of depression: Systematic review and meta-analysis	*BMJ*. 2025 Feb 10;388:r111. doi: 10.1136/bmj.r111.	No
40563744	Palmer C	The potential role of psilocybin in traumatic brain injury recovery: A narrative review	*Brain Sci*. 2025 May 26;15(6):572. doi: 10.3390/brainsci15060572.	No

Notes:

- Search conducted on *11 June 2025*
- Search terms: (*"psilocybin"*[Title]) AND (*"review"*[Title])
- No date range of citations
- Language of citations: *English*

Appendix 2: Studies reviewed by Dawood Hristova and Pérez-Jover 2023

Table 1 Authors, objectives, conditions, designs, participants, and treatments of the studies

Author	Objective	Condition [1]	Design	Participants	Treatment
Ross et al., 2016	To study the effects of psilocybin therapy on cancer patients with depressive and anxious symptoms.	D&A	Double-blind, controlled, randomised, crossover	- Group 1 (first placebo/second psilocybin): N = 15 (27% men, 73% women).Mean age: 60.27- Group 2 (first psilocybin/ second placebo): N = 14 (50% men, 50% women).Mean age: 52- Total N = 29 (18 men, 11 women). Mean age: 56.28	Three preparatory sessions (4 weeks) to establish therapeutic alliance. Then, two dosing sessions (alternating psilocybin or placebo) with psychotherapy separated by 7 weeks, supported by therapists with a non-directive and supportive attitude. Between doses, three integration sessions (total of 6 h) were conducted. Finally, three additional integrative sessions (total of 6 h) were conducted after the second dose, over a period of 6 weeks.

(continued)

(continued)

Carhart-Harris et al., 2016	To study the feasibility, safety, and efficacy of psilocybin in patients with major depressive disorder.	MDD (TR)	Open-label	N = 12(6 men, 6 women).Mean age: 42.7	One preparatory session (4 h), followed by two doses with music therapy, separated by one week. After each dose, an integrative session was conducted.
Giffiths et al., 2016	To study the effects of psilocybin therapy on cancer patients with depressive and anxious symptoms.	D&A	Double-blind, controlled, randomised, crossover	- Group 1 (first high dose/second low dose): N = 25 (52% men, 48% women).Mean age: 56.1- Group 2 (first low dose/ second high dose): N = 26 (50% men, 50% women).Mean age: 56.5- Total N = 51 (51% men, 49% women).Mean age: 56.3	Three preparatory sessions, followed by two doses of psilocybin (alternating high and low) separated by 5 weeks, and six sessions for dialogue and analysis of the experience with psilocybin (three between doses and three after the second dose).
Lyons & Carhart-Harris, 2018	To investigate the effects of a psilocybin intervention on pessimistic biases in patients with treatment-resistant depression.	MDD (TR)	Open-label, controlled trial (mixed model)	- Control group (healthy): N = 15 (60% men, 40% women). Mean age: 37.6- Experimental group (depressed): N = 15 (73.3% men, 26.7% women).Mean age: 45.4- Total N = 30 (66.7% men, 33.3% women). Mean age: 41.5	One preparatory session (4 h), followed by two doses with music therapy, separated by one week. After each dose, an integrative session was conducted.
Carhart-Harris et al., 2018	To study the efficacy and safety of psilocybin therapy for depression over a period of 6 months.	MDD (TR)	Open-label	N = 20 (14 men, 6 women).Mean age: 42.2	One preparatory session (4 h), followed by two doses with music therapy, separated by one week. After each dose, an integrative session was conducted.

(continued)

(continued)

Carhart-Harris et al., 2021	To compare psilocybin treatment with escitalopram treatment.	D&A	Double-blind, controlled randomised	- Escitalopram group: N = 29 (20 men, 9 women). Mean age: 39.1- Psilocybin group: N = 30 (19 men, 11 women). Mean age: 43.3- Total N = 59 (39 men, 20 women). Mean age: 41.2	Six weeks of treatment with six sessions: the first one for preparation before the first dose; the second one for taking the first dose; the third one for exploring the experience during the first dose; the fourth one for taking the second dose; the fifth one for psychological integration of the doses; and the sixth one for exploring the treatment experience.
Davis et al., 2021	To investigate the effect of psilocybin therapy in patients with major depressive disorder.	D&A	Controlled, randomised	- First group (immediate treatment): N = 13 (5 men, 9 women). Mean age: 43.6- Second group (delayed treatment): N = 11 (4 men, 7 women). Mean age: 35.2- Total N = 24 (8 men, 16 women). Mean age: 39.8	Eight weeks of intervention: three weeks of preparatory sessions for the doses (8 h total), two sessions with doses in weeks 3 and 4 of treatment along with music therapy, and two integration sessions (2–3 h) after each dose. One group received immediate treatment with psilocybin, and the other received treatment after 8 weeks (at the end of the first group), to differentiate the psilocybin intervention from spontaneous improvement.

(continued)

(continued)

Gukasyan et al., 2022	To study the efficacy and safety of psilocybin therapy over 12 months.	D&A	Controlled, randomised	- First group (immediate treatment): N = 13 (5 men, 9 women). Mean age: 43.6- Second group (delayed treatment): N = 11 (4 men, 7 women). Mean age: 35.2- Total N = 24 (8 men, 16 women). Mean age: 39.8	Eight weeks of intervention: three weeks of preparatory sessions for the doses (8 h in total), two sessions with doses in weeks 3 and 4 of treatment along with music therapy, and two integration sessions (2–3 h) after each dose. One group underwent immediate treatment with psilocybin, and the other group underwent treatment after 8 weeks (at the end of the first group's treatment), to differentiate psilocybin intervention from spontaneous improvement.

Source: Dawood Hristova & Pérez-Jover, 2023, pp. 5–6

Table 2 Dosage, measurement instruments, results, and conclusions of the studies

Author	Dosage	Measurement Instruments[1]	Results	Conclusion
Ross et al., 2016	0.3 mg/kg psilocybin or 250 mg niacin (placebo)	- HADS-D- BDI	Group 2 had a more significant reduction in symptoms than Group 1 in HADS-D scores 1 day, 2, 6, and 7 weeks after the first dose ($d = 1.23$ ($p \leq 0.001$), $d = 1.12$ ($p \leq 0.01$), $d = 1.32$ ($p \leq 0.001$), and $d = 0.98$ ($p \leq 0.001$), respectively). The results in the BDI measure were similar ($d = 1.10$ ($p \leq 0.01$), $d = 0.99$ ($p \leq 0.01$), $d = 1.07$ ($p \leq 0.01$), and $d = 0.82$ ($p \leq 0.05$)). Group 1 showed significant results after crossing over to the second dose for up to 8 months, with a symptom remission rate of 60% in BDI and HADS-D. Group 2 had a more stable symptom remission rate throughout the treatment, ultimately reaching 80% in both instruments.	Psychotherapy and a moderate dose of psilocybin produce a rapid and prolonged antidepressant response, which can last from 7 weeks to 8 months. The administration of psilocybin with proper psychotherapy could become a novel treatment for cancer-related depression.
Carhart-Harris et al., 2016	Dose 1: 10 mg psilocybin;Dose 2: 25 mg psilocybin	- HAM-D- QIDS- BDI- MADRS	The QIDS scores showed a significant decrease in symptoms from baseline (M = 19.2 (2.0)) with a maximum reduction at 2 weeks (M = 6.3 (4.6); $g = 3.2$, $p = 0.002$) and up to 3 months (M = 10.0 (6.0); $g = 2.0$, $p = 0.003$) after the last dose.The scores also decreased considerably one week after the last dose in BDI (33.7 (7.1) vs. 8.7 (8.4); $g = 3.2$, $p = 0.002$),in HAM-D (21.4 (4.5) vs. 7.4 (6.9); $g = 2.4$, $p = 0.003$) andin MADRS (31 (5) vs. 9.7 (9.8); $g = 2.7$, $p = 0.002$).	Psilocybin has a novel pharmacological action compared to current depression treatments. Hence, it could be a useful adjunct to therapies for this disorder.

(continued)

(continued)

Author	Dosage	Measurement Instruments[1]	Results	Conclusion
Giffiths et al., 2016	High dose of psilocybin: 22 mg/70 kg; Low dose of psilocybin (placebo):1 mg/70 kg	- GRID-GRID-HAMD-17-BDI	The scores of the GRID-HAMD-17 measure reflected a significant reduction in group 1 after the first dose compared to baseline (22.84 (0.97) vs. 6.64 (1.04); $p < 0.001$), unlike group 2 (22.32 (0.88) vs. 14.80 (1.45)). These scores were similar after the crossover in the second dose, remaining constant for up to 6 months (6.95 (1.24), $p < 0.001$ in group 1 and 6.23 (1.30); $p < 0.001$ in group 2, with a combined effect size of $d = 2.98$). The results of the BDI instrument after the first dose also favoured group 1 (17.77 (1.61) vs. 7 (1.39); $p < 0.01$) compared to group 2 (18.40 (1.09) vs. 12.92 (1.58) with a combined effect size), remaining similar at 6 months with a combined effect size of $d = 1.63$ ($p < 0.001$).	Therapy with a single dose of psilocybin produces a substantial and enduring decrease in depressive mood, at least up to 6 months.

(continued)

(continued)

Author	Dosage	Measurement Instruments[1]	Results	Conclusion
Lyons & Carhart-Harris, 2018	Dose 1: 10 mg psilocybin;Dose 2: 25 mg psilocybin	- BDI, 1961)- POFLE	There was a significant reduction in BDI scores in the experimental group from baseline to 1 week after the last dose (M = 34.33 (7.44) vs. 12.13 (9.8); $g = 1.9, p < 0.001$) compared to the control group(M = 3.67 (3.83) vs. 2.73 (3.41); $p = 0.284$). According to the results of the POFLE measure, the experimental group made a similar prediction of desirable and undesirable future events (M = 0.29 (0.15) vs. M = 0.23 (0.15); $p = 0.317$, respectively), but ultimately had more desirable than undesirable events (M = 4.6 (1.76)) vs. M = 1.4 (1.35); $g = 1.5$, $p < 0.001$). The control group predictions of desirable and undesirable events (M = 0.57 (0.09) vs. M = 0.22 (0.16); $g = 2.0, p < 0.001$) were more realistic, ultimately resulting in more desirable than undesirable events (M = 5.6 (1.45) vs. M = 2.23 (1.84); $g = 1.2$, $p < 0.001$).	The findings suggest that psilocybin therapy may decrease pessimistic traits and give patients a more accurate and realistic perspective of their future.

(continued)

(continued)

Author	Dosage	Measurement Instruments[1]	Results	Conclusion
Carhart-Harris et al., 2018	Dose 1: 10 mg psilocybin;Dose 2: 25 mg psilocybin	- QIDS-SR16- BDI- SHAPS- HAM-D	QIDS-SR16 scores were significantly reduced at 1, 2, 3, 5 weeks, and 3 months post-treatment ($d = 2.2$, 2.2, 2.1, 2.3, and 1.5 ($p < 0.001$), respectively).HAM-D scores had a significant reduction in scores at 1 week post-treatment (24.1 (5.4) vs. 9.3 (7.6); $d = 2.3$, $p < 0.001$). BDI scores were significantly reduced at 1 week, 3 months, and 6 months ($d = 2.5$, 1.4, and 1.4 ($p < 0.001$), respectively).SHAPS scores were also significantly reduced at 1 week post-treatment ($d = 1.3$, $p < 0.001$) and at 3 months ($d = 0.8$, $p < 0.005$).	Two sessions with psilocybin produced a rapid and significant improvement in depressive symptoms, which was maintained for up to 6 months post-treatment. This substance represents a promising paradigm for treatment-resistant depression.
Carhart-Harris et al., 2021	25 or 1 mg of psilocybin in the dosing sessions. Daily capsule consumption, placebo for the psilocybin group and 10 mg of escitalopram for the comparison group. After the second dosing session, the escitalopram consumption was doubled (20 mg) for 3 weeks.	- QIDS	In the sixth week of treatment, there were no significant differences in QIDS scores between the psilocybin and escitalopram groups (−8.0 (1.0) vs. −6.0 (1.0), $p = 0.17$, respectively). In that week, 21 patients (70%) in the psilocybin group and 14 patients (48%) in the escitalopram group showed a treatment response (without a significant difference). Remission of symptoms was also observed in 17 patients (57%) in the psilocybin group and 8 (28%) in the escitalopram group.	According to the QIDS-SR-16 measure, this trial did not show a significant difference in antidepressant effects between psilocybin and escitalopram.

(continued)

(continued)

Author	Dosage	Measurement Instruments[1]	Results	Conclusion
Davis et al., 2021	Dose 1 (moderate–high): 20 mg/70 kg psilocybin;Dose 2 (high): 30 mg/70 kg psilocybin	- GRID-HAMD-QIDS	The scores of the GRID-HAMD measure in the first group significantly improved from baseline (22.9 (3.6)) to 1 week (8.0 (7.1); $d = 2.3$, $p < 0.001$) and 4 weeks (8.5 (5.7); $d = 2.3$, $p < 0.001$) after the second dose.The scores of the QIDS measure also had a significant decrease from baseline to 1 day after the first dose (16.7 (3.5) vs. 6.3 (4.4); $d = 2.6$, $p < 0.001$) and remained until 4 weeks after the second dose (6.0 (5.7); $d = 2.3$, $p < 0.001$). The scores of the second group remained constant before their respective treatment.	The results demonstrate that psilocybin therapy is a fast, sustainable way to treat major depressive disorder.
Gukasyan et al., 2022	Dose 1 (moderate–high): 20 mg/70 kg psilocybin;Dose 2 (high): 30 mg/70 kg psilocybin	- GRID-HAMD-QIDS- BDI-II	The mean scores on GRID-HAMD in the overall sample gradually decreased at 3, 6, and 12 months post-treatment, all showing significant differences ($p < 0.001$) with very large effect sizes ($d = 2.0$, 2.6, and 2.4, respectively).The rates of symptom remission on the QIDS measure were generally consistent at these time points (58%, 67%, and 67%, respectively), as were those on the BDI-II (58%, 75%, and 75%, respectively).	The psilocybin-assisted treatment for depression produced considerable antidepressant effects up to 12 months post-treatment.

Source: Dawood Hristova & Pérez-Jover, 2023, pp. 8–10

References

Carhart-Harris, R. L., Bolstridge, M., Day, C. M. J., Rucker, J., Watts, R., Erritzoe, D. E., Kaelen, M., Giribaldi, B., Bloomfield, M., Pilling, S., Rickard, J. A., Forbes, B., Feilding, A., Taylor, D., Curran, H. V., & Nutt, D. J. (2018). Psilocybin with psychological support for treatment-resistant depression: six-month follow-up. *Psychopharmacology*, *235*(2), 399–408. https://doi.org/10.1007/s00213-017-4771-x

Carhart-Harris, R. L., Bolstridge, M., Rucker, J., Day, C. M., Erritzoe, D., Kaelen, M., Bloomfield, M., Rickard, J. A., Forbes, B., Feilding, A., Taylor, D., Pilling, S., Curran, V. H., & Nutt, D. J. (2016). Psilocybin with psychological support for treatment-resistant depression: an open-label feasibility study. *The Lancet. Psychiatry*, *3*(7), 619–627. https://doi.org/10.1016/S2215-0366(16)30065-7

Carhart-Harris, R., Giribaldi, B., Watts, R., Baker-Jones, M., Murphy-Beiner, A., Murphy, R., Martell, J., Blemings, A., Erritzoe, D., & Nutt, D. J. (2021). Trial of Psilocybin versus Escitalopram for Depression. *The New England Journal of Medicine*, *384*(15), 1402–1411. https://doi.org/10.1056/NEJMoa2032994

Davis, A. K., Barrett, F. S., May, D. G., Cosimano, M. P., Sepeda, N. D., Johnson, M. W., Finan, P. H., & Griffiths, R. R. (2021). Effects of Psilocybin-Assisted Therapy on Major Depressive Disorder: A Randomized Clinical Trial. *JAMA Psychiatry*, *78*(5), 481–489. https://doi.org/10.1001/jamapsychiatry.2020.3285

Griffiths, R. R., Johnson, M. W., Carducci, M. A., Umbricht, A., Richards, W. A., Richards, B. D., Cosimano, M. P., & Klinedinst, M. A. (2016). Psilocybin produces substantial and sustained decreases in depression and anxiety in patients with life-threatening cancer: A randomized double-blind trial. *Journal of Psychopharmacology (Oxford, England)*, *30*(12), 1181–1197. https://doi.org/10.1177/0269881116675513

Gukasyan, N., Davis, A. K., Barrett, F. S., Cosimano, M. P., Sepeda, N. D., Johnson, M. W., & Griffiths, R. R. (2022). Efficacy and safety of psilocybin-assisted treatment for major depressive disorder: Prospective 12-month follow-up. *Journal of Psychopharmacology (Oxford, England)*, *36*(2), 151–158. https://doi.org/10.1177/02698811211073759

Lyons, T., & Carhart-Harris, R. L. (2018). More Realistic Forecasting of Future Life Events After Psilocybin for Treatment-Resistant Depression. *Frontiers in Psychology*, *9*, 1721. https://doi.org/10.3389/fpsyg.2018.01721

Ross, S., Bossis, A., Guss, J., Agin-Liebes, G., Malone, T., Cohen, B., Mennenga, S. E., Belser, A., Kalliontzi, K., Babb, J., Su, Z., Corby, P., & Schmidt, B. L. (2016). Rapid and sustained symptom reduction following psilocybin treatment for anxiety and depression in patients with life-threatening cancer: a randomized controlled trial. *Journal of Psychopharmacology (Oxford, England)*, *30*(12), 1165–1180. https://doi.org/10.1177/0269881116675512

Appendix 3: Studies Reviewed by Li et al. 2024

Table 1 Psilocybin for depression: clinical efficacy

Studies	Assessment scales	Findings
The severity of depressive symptoms		
Carhart-Harris et al., 2021	BDI, HAMD-17, MADRS and QIDS-SR-16	Psilocybin was more effective than escitalopram at week 6 in improving depressive symptoms as measured by the BDI, HAMD-17, and MADRS (secondary outcomes) but not the QIDS-SR-16 (primary outcome).
Davis et al., 2021	BDI, HAMD-17, QIDS-SR-16 and PHQ-9	Psilocybin significantly improved depressive symptoms as measured by the BDI, HAMD-17, QIDS-SR-16, and PHQ-9 at weeks 1 and 4 post-session 2.
Goodwin et al., 2022	MADRS	Psilocybin, at a single dose of 25 mg, but not 10 mg, significantly improved depressive symptoms more than a 1 mg dose, as measured by the MADRS at day 2 and weeks 1 and 3. Improvement in depressive symptoms at weeks 6, 9, and 12 between the 25 mg group or the 10 mg group and the 1 mg group, as measured by the MADRS showed no significant differences.
Raison et al., 2023	MADRS	Psilocybin was significantly superior to niacin in improving depressive symptoms on the MADRS at weeks 1, 2, 4, and 6.
von Rotz et al., 2023	BDI and MADRS	Psilocybin was significantly more effective than a placebo in improving depressive symptoms as measured by the BDI and MADRS at days 0, 2, and weeks 1, 2.
The severity of anxiety symptoms		
Carhart-Harris et al., 2021	STAI	Psilocybin was more effective than escitalopram at week 6 in improving anxiety symptoms as measured by the STAI.
Davis et al., 2021	HAMA and STAI	Psilocybin significantly improved anxiety symptoms as measured by the HAMA and STAI at week 4 post-session 2.
Goodwin et al., 2022	NR	NR
Raison et al., 2023	HAMA	Psilocybin was significantly more effective than niacin in improving anxiety symptoms on the HAMA at weeks 1, 2, 4, and 6.
von Rotz et al., 2023	HAMA	Psilocybin was significantly more effective than a placebo in improving anxiety symptoms as measured by the HAMA at week 2.
The severity of suicidal ideation		
Carhart-Harris et al., 2021	SIDAS	Psilocybin was more effective than escitalopram at week 6 in reducing suicidal ideation as measured by the SIDAS.
Davis et al., 2021	C-SSRS	Psilocybin did not significantly reduce suicidal ideation as measured by the C-SSRS.

(continued)

(continued)

Studies	Assessment scales	Findings
The severity of suicidal ideation		
Goodwin et al., 2022	FDA-CASA 2012	Suicidal ideation occurred in all dose groups, and no significant differences were observed between the three dose groups as measured by the FDA-CASA 2012.
Raison et al., 2023	C-SSRS	No significant group differences between psilocybin and niacin in reducing suicidal ideation as measured by the C-SSRS.
von Rotz et al., 2023	C-SSRS	No significant group differences between psilocybin and placebo in reducing suicidal ideation as measured by the C-SSRS.

Notes: *BDI* Beck Depression Inventory, *C-SSRS* Colombia-Suicidality severity rating scale, *FDACASA* Food and Drug Administration Classification Algorithm of Suicide Assessment, conversion of C-SSRS and S-STS (Sheehan Suicidality Tracking Scale), *HAMD-17* 17-item Hamilton Depression Rating Scale, *HAMA* Hamilton Anxiety Rating Scale, *MADRS* Montgomery-Åsberg Depression Rating Scale, *NR* not reported, *NS*—not significant, *PHQ-9* 9-item Patient Health Questionnaire, *QIDS-SR-16* 16-item Quick Inventory of Depressive Symptomatology-Self Report, *SIDAS* Suicidal Ideation Attributes Scale, *STAI* Spielberger's Trait Anxiety Inventory
Source: Li et al., 2024, p. 6

References

Carhart-Harris, R., Giribaldi, B., Watts, R., Baker-Jones, M., Murphy-Beiner, A., Murphy, R., Martell, J., Blemings, A., Erritzoe, D., & Nutt, D. J. (2021). Trial of Psilocybin versus Escitalopram for Depression. *The New England Journal of Medicine*, *384*(15), 1402–1411. https://doi.org/10.1056/NEJMoa2032994

Davis, A. K., Barrett, F. S., May, D. G., Cosimano, M. P., Sepeda, N. D., Johnson, M. W., Finan, P. H., & Griffiths, R. R. (2021). Effects of Psilocybin-Assisted Therapy on Major Depressive Disorder: A Randomized Clinical Trial. *JAMA Psychiatry*, *78*(5), 481–489. https://doi.org/10.1001/jamapsychiatry.2020.3285

Goodwin, G. M., Aaronson, S. T., Alvarez, O., Arden, P. C., Baker, A., Bennett, J. C., Bird, C., Blom, R. E., Brennan, C., Brusch, D., Burke, L., Campbell-Coker, K., Carhart-Harris, R., Cattell, J., Daniel, A., DeBattista, C., Dunlop, B. W., Eisen, K., Feifel, D., Forbes, M., … Malievskaia, E. (2022). Single-Dose Psilocybin for a Treatment-Resistant Episode of Major Depression. *The New England Journal of Medicine*, *387*(18), 1637–1648. https://doi.org/10.1056/NEJMoa2206443

Raison, C. L., Sanacora, G., Woolley, J., Heinzerling, K., Dunlop, B. W., Brown, R. T., Kakar, R., Hassman, M., Trivedi, R. P., Robison, R., Gukasyan, N., Nayak, S. M., Hu, X., O'Donnell, K. C., Kelmendi, B., Sloshower, J., Penn, A. D., Bradley, E., Kelly, D. F., Mletzko, T., et al. (2023). Single-Dose Psilocybin Treatment for Major Depressive Disorder: A Randomized Clinical Trial. *JAMA*, *330*(9), 843–853. https://doi.org/10.1001/jama.2023.14530

von Rotz, R., Schindowski, E. M., Jungwirth, J., Schuldt, A., Rieser, N. M., Zahoranszky, K., Seifritz, E., Nowak, A., Nowak, P., Jäncke, L., Preller, K. H., & Vollenweider, F. X. (2022). Single-dose psilocybin-assisted therapy in major depressive disorder: A placebo-controlled, double-blind, randomised clinical trial. *EClinicalMedicine*, *56*, 101809. https://doi.org/10.1016/j.eclinm.2022.101809

Appendix 4: Studies Reviewed by Salvetti et al. 2024

Table 1 Summary of the characteristics of the studies in which a single-dose psilocybin was used

ID	Study Design	Treatments	Psilocybin Dosage	Control (Dosage)	Clinical Measures	Effects
Goodwin et al., 2022	RCT	Three preparatory meetings, one dose of psilocybin with music, and two psychological integration sessions	10 mg or 25 mg	Psilocybin (1 mg)	MADRS	Mean MADRS scores decreased by 12 points in the first group (25 mg), by 7.9 points in the second group (10 mg), and by 5.4 in the third group (1 mg) at 3 weeks after treatment
Goodwin et al., 2023	Open-label	Three preparatory meetings, one dose of psilocybin with music, and two integration sessions	25 mg	–	MADRS, QIDS	Mean MADRS scores decreased by 14.9 points at week 3 weeks after treatment
Raison et al., 2023	RCT	Preparatory sessions totalling 6–8 h, one dose of psilocybin or niacin with music, followed by 4 h integration sessions	25 mg	Niacin (100 mg)	MADRS	Significant reduction in mean MADRS scores in the treatment group (−19.1) compared to controls (−6.8) from baseline to 43 days after treatment
Sloshower et al., 2023	Placebo-controlled within-subjects	2 h preparatory sessions, a single dose of psilocybin or placebo, and two sessions of psychotherapy	0.3 mg/kg	Placebo	HAMD, QIDS	Greater reduction in mean QIDS scores following psilocybin administration (Δ = 6.3–8.7) than placebo (Δ = 4.4–5.8) at 2 weeks after treatment

(continued)

(continued)

ID	Study Design	Treatments	Psilocybin Dosage	Control (Dosage)	Clinical Measures	Effects
von Rotz et al., 2023	RCT	Two preparatory sessions, one dose of psilocybin or placebo, and three integration sessions	0.215 mg/kg	Placebo	MADRS, BDI	Reduction in mean MADRS scores in the treatment group (−13.2) compared to baseline, with an effect size significantly larger than placebo at 2 weeks after treatment

Notes: *RCT* Randomised Controlled Trial, *BDI* Beck Depression Inventory, *HAMD* Hamilton Depression Rating Scale, *MADRS* Montgomery-Åsberg Depression Rating Scale, *QIDS* Quick Inventory of Depressive Symptomatology
Source: Salvetti et al., 2024, p. 8

Table 2 Summary of the characteristics of the studies in which two doses of psilocybin were used

ID	Study Design	Treatments	First Psilocybin Dosage	Second Psilocybin Dosage	Control (Dosage)	Clinical Measures	Effects
Carhart-Harris et al., 2016	Open-label	Preparatory sessions totalling 4 h, two doses of psilocybin with music, 1-week apart, and two integration sessions	10 mg	25 mg	–	QIDS, BDI, HAMD, MADRS	Decrease in QIDS scores compared to baseline (−11.8) at 1 week after treatment. A further decrement in mean QIDS scores (−9.2) was observed at 3-month follow-up
Carhart-Harris et al., 2017	Open-label	Preparatory sessions totalling 4 h, two doses of psilocybin with music, 1-week apart, and two integration sessions	10 mg	25 mg	–	QIDS	Reduced QIDS scores compared to baseline (−8.0) at 5 weeks after treatment
Carhart-Harris et al., 2018	Open-label	Preparatory sessions totalling 4 h, two doses of psilocybin with music, 1-week apart. After each dose, an integrative session was conducted	10 mg	25 mg	–	QIDS, BDI, HAMD	Reduction in mean QIDS scores compared to baseline at 1 week, 2 weeks, 3 weeks, 5 weeks, and 3 months after treatment. BDI scores were significantly lower compared to baseline at 1 week, 3 months, and 6 months after treatment
Lyons and Carhart-Harris, 2018	Open-label	Preparatory sessions totalling 4 h, two doses of psilocybin with music, 1-week apart, and two integration sessions	10 mg	25 mg	–	BDI, HAMD	Decrease in BDI scores (−22.2) compared to baseline at 1 week after treatment

(continued)

(continued)

Carhart-Harris et al., 2021	RCT	Preparatory sessions totalling 3 h, two doses of psilocybin or escitalopram, 3 weeks apart, and an integrative session	25 mg	25 mg	Psilocybin (1 mg)	QIDS, BDI, HAMD, MADRS	At 6 weeks, the mean QIDS change score compared to baseline was −6.0 in the escitalopram group and −8.0 in the psilocybin group
Davis et al., 2021	Randomised waiting-list	Preparatory sessions totalling 8 h, two doses of psilocybin with music, spaced ~2 weeks apart, and two integration sessions	20 mg	30 mg	Waiting list	HAMD, QIDS	Mean HAMD scores decreased in the immediate treatment group compared to baseline at 1 week (−8.0) and 1 month (8.5) after treatment. Mean HAMD scores remained stable in subjects belonging to the waiting list
Gukasyan et al., 2022	Follow-up	Preparatory sessions totalling 8 h, two doses of psilocybin with music, spaced ~2 weeks apart, and two integration sessions	20 mg	30 mg	–	HAMD, QIDS	Mean HAMD scores decreased in both immediate and delayed treatment groups compared to baseline at 1 week, 1 month, 3 months, 6 months, and 12 months after treatment

Notes: RCT Randomised Controlled Trial, *BDI* Beck Depression Inventory, *HAMD* Hamilton Depression Rating Scale, *MADRS* Montgomery-Åsberg Depression Rating Scale, *QIDS* Quick Inventory of Depressive Symptomatology
Source: Salvetti et al., 2024, p. 10

References

Carhart-Harris, R. L., Bolstridge, M., Day, C. M. J., Rucker, J., Watts, R., Erritzoe, D. E., Kaelen, M., Giribaldi, B., Bloomfield, M., Pilling, S., Rickard, J. A., Forbes, B., Feilding, A., Taylor, D., Curran, H. V., & Nutt, D. J. (2018). Psilocybin with psychological support for treatment-resistant depression: six-month follow-up. *Psychopharmacology*, *235*(2), 399–408. https://doi.org/10.1007/s00213-017-4771-x

Carhart-Harris, R. L., Bolstridge, M., Rucker, J., Day, C. M., Erritzoe, D., Kaelen, M., Bloomfield, M., Rickard, J. A., Forbes, B., Feilding, A., Taylor, D., Pilling, S., Curran, V. H., & Nutt, D. J. (2016). Psilocybin with psychological support for treatment-resistant depression: an open-label feasibility study. *The Lancet. Psychiatry*, *3*(7), 619–627. https://doi.org/10.1016/S2215-0366(16)30065-7

Carhart-Harris, R. L., Roseman, L., Bolstridge, M., Demetriou, L., Pannekoek, J. N., Wall, M. B., Tanner, M., Kaelen, M., McGonigle, J., Murphy, K., Leech, R., Curran, H. V., & Nutt, D. J. (2017). Psilocybin for treatment-resistant depression: fMRI-measured brain mechanisms. *Scientific Reports*, *7*(1), 13187. https://doi.org/10.1038/s41598-017-13282-7

Carhart-Harris, R., Giribaldi, B., Watts, R., Baker-Jones, M., Murphy-Beiner, A., Murphy, R., Martell, J., Blemings, A., Erritzoe, D., & Nutt, D. J. (2021). Trial of Psilocybin versus Escitalopram for Depression. *The New England Journal of Medicine*, *384*(15), 1402–1411. https://doi.org/10.1056/NEJMoa2032994

Davis, A. K., Barrett, F. S., May, D. G., Cosimano, M. P., Sepeda, N. D., Johnson, M. W., Finan, P. H., & Griffiths, R. R. (2021). Effects of Psilocybin-Assisted Therapy on Major Depressive Disorder: A Randomized Clinical Trial. *JAMA Psychiatry*, *78*(5), 481–489. https://doi.org/10.1001/jamapsychiatry.2020.3285

Goodwin, G. M., Aaronson, S. T., Alvarez, O., Arden, P. C., Baker, A., Bennett, J. C., Bird, C., Blom, R. E., Brennan, C., Brusch, D., Burke, L., Campbell-Coker, K., Carhart-Harris, R., Cattell, J., Daniel, A., DeBattista, C., Dunlop, B. W., Eisen, K., Feifel, D., Forbes, M., … & Malievskaia, E. (2022). Single-Dose Psilocybin for a Treatment-Resistant Episode of Major Depression. *The New England Journal of Medicine*, *387*(18), 1637–1648. https://doi.org/10.1056/NEJMoa2206443

Goodwin, G. M., Croal, M., Feifel, D., Kelly, J. R., Marwood, L., Mistry, S., O'Keane, V., Peck, S. K., Simmons, H., Sisa, C., Stansfield, S. C., Tsai, J., Williams, S., & Malievskaia, E. (2023). Psilocybin for treatment resistant depression in patients taking a concomitant SSRI medication. *Neuropsychopharmacology: Official publication of the American College of Neuropsychopharmacology*, *48*(10), 1492–1499. https://doi.org/10.1038/s41386-023-01648-7

Gukasyan, N., Davis, A. K., Barrett, F. S., Cosimano, M. P., Sepeda, N. D., Johnson, M. W., & Griffiths, R. R. (2022). Efficacy and safety of psilocybin-assisted treatment for major depressive disorder: Prospective 12-month follow-up. *Journal of Psychopharmacology (Oxford, England)*, *36*(2), 151–158. https://doi.org/10.1177/02698811211073759

Lyons, T., & Carhart-Harris, R. L. (2018). More Realistic Forecasting of Future Life Events After Psilocybin for Treatment-Resistant Depression. *Frontiers in Psychology*, *9*, 1721. https://doi.org/10.3389/fpsyg.2018.01721

Raison, C. L., Sanacora, G., Woolley, J., Heinzerling, K., Dunlop, B. W., Brown, R. T., Kakar, R., Hassman, M., Trivedi, R. P., Robison, R., Gukasyan, N., Nayak, S. M., Hu, X., O'Donnell, K. C., Kelmendi, B., Sloshower, J., Penn, A. D., Bradley, E., Kelly, D. F., Mletzko, T., … Griffiths, R. R. (2023). Single-Dose Psilocybin Treatment for Major Depressive Disorder: A Randomized Clinical Trial. *JAMA*, *330*(9), 843–853. https://doi.org/10.1001/jama.2023.14530

Sloshower, J., Skosnik, P. D., Safi-Aghdam, H., Pathania, S., Syed, S., Pittman, B., & D'Souza, D. C. (2023). Psilocybin-assisted therapy for major depressive disorder: An exploratory placebo-controlled, fixed-order trial. *Journal of Psychopharmacology (Oxford, England)*, *37*(7), 698–706. https://doi.org/10.1177/02698811231154852

von Rotz, R., Schindowski, E. M., Jungwirth, J., Schuldt, A., Rieser, N. M., Zahoranszky, K., Seifritz, E., Nowak, A., Nowak, P., Jäncke, L., Preller, K. H., & Vollenweider, F. X. (2022). Single-dose psilocybin-assisted therapy in major depressive disorder: A placebo-controlled, double-blind, randomised clinical trial. *EClinicalMedicine*, *56*, 101809. https://doi.org/10.1016/j.eclinm.2022.101809

MIX
Papier aus verantwortungsvollen Quellen
Paper from responsible sources
FSC® C105338

If you have any concerns about our products,
you can contact us on
ProductSafety@springernature.com

In case Publisher is established outside the EU,
the EU authorized representative is:
Springer Nature Customer Service Center GmbH
Europaplatz 3, 69115 Heidelberg, Germany

Printed by Libri Plureos GmbH
in Hamburg, Germany